Investing Duplexes, Triplexes & Quads

The Fastest and *Safest* Way to Real Estate Wealth

Larry B. Loftis, Esq.

KAPLAN) PUBLISHING

President, Kaplan Publishing: Roy Lipner
Vice President and Publisher: Maureen McMahon
Acquisitions Editor: Victoria Smith
Senior Managing Editor: Jack Kiburz
Typesetter: Todd Bowman
Cover Designer: DePinto Studios

Published by Kaplan Publishing,
a division of Kaplan, Inc.

Printed in the United States of America

17

Library of Congress Cataloging-in-Publication Data

Loftis, Larry B.
  Investing in duplexes, triplexes, and quads : the fastest and safest way to real estate wealth / Larry B. Loftis, Esq.
      p. cm.
  Includes index.
  ISBN-13: 978-1-4195-3725-7
  ISBN-10: 1-4195-3725-3
  1. Real estate investment–United States. 2. Apartment houses–Purchasing–United States. 3. Residential real estate–Purchasing–United States. I. Title.
  HD259.L635 2006
  332.63'243–dc22

                                   2006002419

For information about ordering Kaplan Publishing books at special quantity discounts, please call 1-800-KAP-ITEM or write to Kaplan Publishing, 888 Seventh Avenue, 22nd floor, New York, NY 10106.

DEDICATION

For Bob Baird, the consummate professional and a great friend.

Contents

As I write this, the United States is on the heels of one of the largest real estate booms in history. Fueled by the lowest interest rates in 40 years, millions of Americans who once were unable to afford mortgage payments have purchased their first homes. Others have taken advantage of low mortgage rates and purchased investment properties. In addition, the bear market of the early 2000s forced unsatisfied stock investors into the real estate market. Like other commodities, real estate is ruled by supply and demand economics, which caused property prices to soar in recent years. According to third-quarter 2005 data released from the National Association of Realtors (NAR), existing homes nationwide have appreciated an average of 23 percent over the past two years, and 32 percent over the last three years. The top 20 metropolitan markets saw an average three-year gain of 79 percent. Many real estate investors made a killing.

But the Federal Reserve Board has increased the federal funds rate—its target for the overnight lending rate between banks (which determines the prime rate and mortgage rates)— 13 consecutive times, including 8 times in 2005. Most recently, the federal funds rate increased to 4.25 percent on December 13, 2005. Many prognosticators warned that the real estate "bubble" was about to burst. Some suggested a real estate collapse. Although the real estate market has cooled nationally, no one witnessed a bubble burst. Prices haven't dropped by 20 percent, as some warned, but instead have stabilized.

The research division of the NAR completed a study of 135 U.S. markets in November 2005 and concluded that neither these markets nor the nation as a whole is poised for a housing bust. In fact, the study suggests that most local housing markets are in excellent shape, with potential for significant housing equity gains, particularly over the long run. In some hot areas, demand has normalized. In my market, Orlando, it was common in 2004–2005 for buyers of both residential and multifamily properties to pay *more* than the asking price. According to the Orlando Regional Realtors Association, the median price of existing homes rose an average of 25.4 percent from January 2005 to January 2006 (and 27 percent from December 2004 to December 2005). But in the last quarter of 2005, property sales and prices returned to more normal patterns.

What will happen to the real estate market in the third and fourth quarters of 2006 and in 2007? I honestly don't know. I suspect that prices will stabilize where they are and we'll move back to more historic appreciation rates for the next few years. On February 7, 2006, the NAR's chief economist, David Lereah, stated that home sales can be sustained at current levels and forecasted 2006 to be the third strongest year on record. However, NAR projects that the national median existing-home price and new-home price will increase only 5.0 and 5.7 percent, respectively. If these figures turn out to be accurate, short-term real estate investors won't be making a killing in 12–24 months. At least they won't if they are investing in "normal" properties (i.e., properties not in "hot" or quickly appreciating areas).

This brings me to the underlying question—is it easier to make money in real estate in a hot or soft market, in a buyer's or seller's market? The answer is "yes." What many potential investors fail to see is that market forces "equalize" as interest rates move. For example, when interest rates are low, money is easier to acquire, banks are more lenient in their lending requirements to compete for customers, and many apartment dwellers can afford the mortgage payment for a home. This results in more buyers, thereby increasing demand (while supply remains constant). Increased demand results in price inflation.

This scenario is what we've witnessed over the last five years. Virtually everyone who owned real estate in the last few years made money (or gained equity). I have a friend who bought her first home, a modest three-bedroom, two-bath house on the outskirts of Orlando, in March 2003 for $133,000. By November 2005, comparable sales put the value of her home at over $265,000. In 32 months, she gained about $132,000 in equity. My properties have skyrocketed in value as well. The rising tide lifts all ships, as they say.

But can you make money when the real estate market is down, or when interest rates are high? The answer is not only "yes," but "of course." When the real estate market is down, when it's a buyer's market, sellers outnumber buyers. As a result, sellers must decrease their asking price, sometimes far below the fair market value, if they want to sell their property quickly. Buyers don't have to wait for inflation to give them equity in their properties; they walk into it. In addition, when interest rates are high, sellers are forced to offer seller financing on more reasonable terms. For example, when the prime rate hit 21.5 percent in 1981, sellers were forced to carry back a mortgage on reasonable terms if they wanted to sell their properties.

As you can see, investors can and *do* make money in real estate, regardless of the market or the economy. They just do it in different ways. I can't predict what the real estate market will do in the next five or ten years. What I do know is that the value of real estate will continue up over time. That upward trend has been consistent for over 40 years. And if you learn how to invest in real estate in any market, you will build real wealth over time.

My personal belief is that the *fastest* way to real estate wealth is through investing in residential two- to four-unit multifamily properties. It is also the *safest* way to invest in real estate. As you read, you'll see that investing in these types of properties requires less money and has fewer risks than other types of properties. I'll also show you why banks prefer to lend on these types of properties over commercial properties (five units or more). Finally, the numbers work best in residential multifamily units, where your upside potential is greatest, in my experience. And best of all, anyone can do it.

I hope this book will help you on your journey.

Larry Loftis
March 2006

ACKNOWLEDGMENTS

I would like to thank Vicki Smith, my editor, for her consistent encouragement, and the entire team at Kaplan (Al Martin, Leslie Banks, Julie Marshall, and Jack Kiburz) for their tremendous work. Thanks to Mary Good for her comments and encouragement, and to Gemma Dela Rosa for always helping me to manage properties. Thanks also to Cynthia Scholz and Nicole Incinelli for helping with the cover design and layout. Finally, I owe a great debt of gratitude to Bob Baird, my mortgage broker, for arranging financing on all of my deals and just being a great professional and a wonderful friend.

REAL ESTATE
WEALTH BUILDING

1

WHY REAL ESTATE?

Buy land. They've stopped making it.

—Mark Twain

For the majority of people, real estate is the single best tool for wealth building. For the average person, real estate may be the *only* vehicle to carry him or her to retirement wealth. Sure, one of the best ways to become wealthy is to build your own business. After all, that's what Bill Gates and Michael Dell did. And the owner of the car dealership down the street is doing fairly well, right? And isn't the owner of the McDonald's franchise downtown making big bucks? Without a doubt, building a business can be very lucrative. But how many people possess the money or skills to be able to create and build a multi-million-dollar business? Can the average person do it?

How many people have the genius of a Bill Gates or a Michael Dell? And have you checked to see the latest price tag for buying a car dealership or a McDonald's franchise? Typically, those businesses are bought for upwards of $500,000 to $1,000,000. Oh, and the franchisor wants you to work actively in the business 50 hours a week. Can you start your own business? Sure. But according to the Small Business Administration, 95 percent of new businesses fail in the first three years.

You've probably heard the quote that 75 percent of millionaires made their money through real estate. I don't know if that statistic is true, but all the wealthy people I know either made their money through real estate or sold a business and invested the proceeds in real estate.

One of the best and most original books I've read in recent years is *Rich Dad, Poor Dad,* by Robert Kiyosaki. In his book, Kiyosaki recounts a story about how Ray Kroc, founder of McDonald's, asks a University of Texas MBA class what business he was in. After a few chuckles, one of the students tells Kroc what he expects: "You're in the hamburger business." Pausing for effect, Kroc responded, "Ladies and gentlemen, I'm not in the hamburger business. My business is real estate." You see, McDonald's is the largest owner of real estate in the world. And if you haven't noticed, these restaurants are typically located on the busiest intersections in town.

So what makes real estate so lucrative? Why do even the wealthiest business owners invest large sums of their money in something that was not originally within their area of expertise? Here's the short answer: Real estate, and *only* real estate, can provide the following benefits:

- Cash flow
- Appreciation
- Tax benefits
- Equity buildup
- Leverage

While I'll delve into these benefits in greater detail in the next few pages, let's briefly recognize each of these five reasons to invest in real estate.

Cash flow is simply the money I make each month from owning an investment property. This benefit is the sum I have left over from rents each month after I pay my expenses and mortgage payment.

Appreciation is the increase in value of a property over time. If I buy a property today for $150,000, it will be worth more 10 years from now.

Tax benefits, principally interest deductions and depreciation, allow a real estate investor to reduce his or her tax liability.

Equity buildup is the gradual reduction of principal that one owes on a mortgage or trust deed loan encumbering a property. If you purchase a house tomorrow, you most likely will finance that purchase with a promissory note to either a bank or the seller. As you make payments over time, the principal owed will decrease until you pay off the loan and own the property free and clear (assuming the note is fully amortized).

Leverage is the beautiful thing that lets you buy a $200,000 property with only $20,000 down (or less). In other words, you get the full use and benefits of a $200,000 asset (including 100 percent of the cash flow, appreciation, tax benefits, and equity buildup), even though you put only 10 percent down, or 5 percent, or perhaps even nothing down. If you buy a stock, a certificate of deposit, an annuity, or gold, for example, you must put down 100 percent of the price to get the full benefits.

What other asset or investment gives you all these benefits? What other investment involves minimal risk, and can be understood and utilized by most people? Because these five benefits are your key to wealth building, let's look at each in more detail.

CASH FLOW

Here's a cash-flow analysis of a property that I recently considered buying. This four-unit building (known as a "quadraplex" or "quad" in these parts) is located just outside of Orlando. The area is quaint, but not really rural. The building sits on a huge lot, bordered by massive and beautiful oak trees. The location of the property is quite good as well—it sits just two blocks from a major college campus. The asking price is only $240,000, which is somewhat low here, even for the outskirts of town. Here's why: The rent for each unit is only $475. The going rate for a decent one-bedroom, one-bath unit in the area is $600 to $650 per month.

The word from the seller's broker was that the rents were low because of poor management by the company handling it. That scenario is very possible. It's also possible that the tenants are long-term tenants who have never had their rents increased, or that the place is trashed inside. Whatever the reason is, it doesn't really matter to me. I know the market here and I know those rents could be higher.

I make a number of calculations to see if a property is acceptable to me, but let's first look at cash flow. Here's the current situation:

4 units rented at $475/each = $1,900 total rents per month (It is fully occupied at this point.)

Expenses (including principal and interest on the loan, taxes, insurance, and maintenance) will be approximately $1,789 per month. This is assuming that I buy it at $240,000 and put 10 percent down.

Thus:

$$Income = \$1,900/month$$
$$Expenses = \$1,789/month$$
$$Positive\ cash\ flow = \$111/month$$

Now before you get all worked up and say, "With only $111 per month, how am I going to get rich doing this?" stay with me. You become wealthy over time by realizing a terrific rate of return on your money. Finance folks call this "return on investment" or ROI.

Assume for the moment that I'm really brain-dead and I never improved the property or increased the rent. I make $111 per month on my $24,000 investment, or $1,200 per year. That's a 5.6 percent cash-on-cash return in a safe and steady investment. Keep in mind, of course, that my return is much greater once I factor in appreciation, tax benefits, and equity buildup. For now, however, let's keep it simple and just look at the cash-on-cash return. Most investors would be thrilled to have a safe and steady 5 percent plus (inflation will add at least another 5 percent, on average) return each and every year.

But let's look at reality. If I purchased this property, I would take it subject to the existing leases. Those leases could be month-to-month or have a certain number of months remaining on a lease term. As each lease term expires, or as tenants move out, I would go in and repaint each unit, clean it up, and increase the rents to the current market rate.

I ran two sets of scenarios. First, I assumed that I'd have to honor the existing rents of $475, on average, for six months after purchase. If the numbers look good and I get a contract on the property, I'll get copies of the existing leases and I'll know exactly when they terminate (the seller or seller's broker will usually tell you the expiration dates, but you must verify these dates with the actual lease agreements). For my immediate calculation, rents for six months amount to $11,400 ($475 × 4 × 6). Now assuming that I can only rerent the units for the lower range of the market, or $600 per unit, that's $14,400 for the next six months. Thus, for the year, I have $25,800 in total rents (assuming no vacancies—it's a rough calculation only). My total expenses for the year are $21,468, so my net income is $4,332. Now my cash-on-cash return is 18.1 percent ($4,332 divided by $24,000). Not too bad. So it looks like this:

Total rents	$25,800
Less total expenses	– 21,468
Net cash flow	$4,332

Net cash flow	$4,332
Divided by invested cash	$24,000 = 18.1% return

Now here's the second scenario that I ran. If all four of the existing leases expire in four months, on average, and I can rerent the units for $625 per unit for the next eight months, that's $7,600 (4 units × $475 × 4 months) plus $20,000 (4 units × $625 × 8 months), or $27,600 for the year. Subtracting the annual expenses of $21,468, that's a net annual cash flow of $6,132. Now what does the return look like?

Total rents	$27,600
Less total expenses	– 21,468
Net cash flow	$6,132

Net cash flow	$6,132
Divided by invested cash	$24,000 = 25.6% return

When you take a cash-on-cash return of 18 percent, or 20 percent, or 25 percent, and you add in other benefits such as appreciation, tax benefits, and equity buildup, your overall return is phenomenal. We'll look at the other benefits in due course. For now, just realize that cash flow alone is sufficient reason to invest in real estate, and provides the seeds to real wealth accumulation.

Did I end up buying this property? No. While the numbers worked, an inspection of the property revealed structural problems with the "piers" (support posts for older houses). I'll cover due diligence safeguards in Chapter 9.

APPRECIATION

Most people associate appreciation of a property only with inflation. However, inflation is just one cause of appreciation. A property also can jump in value because of *demand* appreciation or *forced* appreciation. Let's look at all three reasons a property increases in value: inflation appreciation, demand appreciation, and forced appreciation.

Inflation Appreciation

Can you remember when a soft drink cost a dime or a quarter? Today, most vending machines charge one dollar. The same increase in price has occurred in real estate, only more dramatically so. Figure 1.1 illustrates the increase in the average and median price of a U.S. home over the past 30 years (taken from the month of July). Figures 1.2 and 1.3 show graphically the dramatic rise of average and median U.S. house prices, respectively, over the past 30 years.

Look carefully at these prices and the trend of the chart lines. Is there a discernible pattern? Of course, the pattern of U.S. residential real estate prices is up. With a few slight and momentary downturns, the pattern is always up. According to the Office of Federal Housing Enterprise Oversight (OFHEO) (*http://www.ofheo.gov*), the average house price appreciation in the United States over the past 25 years (period ending June 30, 2005) was 261 percent. Even states that weathered severe housing busts because of oil company failures (i.e., Texas and Oklahoma) have seen house appreciation of almost 100 percent.

These are certainly exciting times for real estate investment. While sources may vary slightly in their numbers, experts agree that we are in the midst of the largest U.S. house price appreciation in more than 25 years. While the Census Bureau lists the

FIGURE 1.1   *U.S. House Prices Over the Past 30 Years*

July	Average Price	Median Price
1975	$ 42,300	$ 38,600
1976	48,000	44,600
1977	53,600	48,600
1978	62,900	54,800
1979	71,900	63,800
1980	76,700	64,000
1981	82,600	69,500
1982	86,500	70,900
1983	89,200	75,200
1984	97,100	80,700
1985	99,400	82,100
1986	116,800	94,100
1987	128,600	105,000
1988	141,300	118,000
1989	140,300	116,000
1990	149,800	118,700
1991	148,200	120,000
1992	137,700	118,000
1993	143,400	123,900
1994	144,400	124,400
1995	154,200	131,000
1996	168,400	144,200
1997	175,500	145,900
1998	179,800	149,900
1999	189,100	158,200
2000	202,200	169,000
2001	209,300	175,000
2002	217,800	175,600
2003	248,400	190,200
2004	279,200	212,400
2005	275,000	215,000

Source: U.S. Census Bureau.

FIGURE 1.2 *Average Price of U.S. Houses Actually Sold*

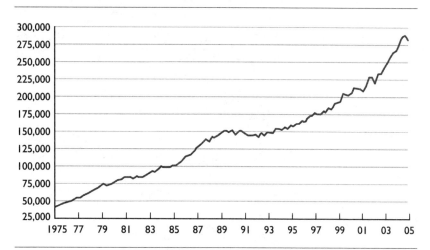

Source: Economic Chart Dispenser, *http://www.Economagic.com.*

FIGURE 1.3 *Median Prices of U.S. Houses Actually Sold*

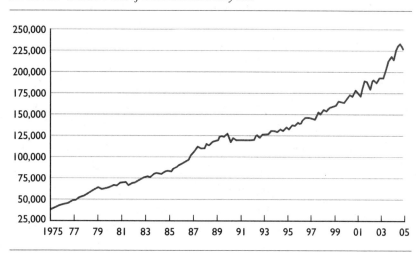

Source: Economic Chart Dispenser, *http://www.Economagic.com.*

median sales price of a U.S. house in July of 2005 as $215,000, the National Association of Realtors (NAR) states that the median sale price for an *existing* home was $219,000 as of June of 2005.

The NAR states that this figure represents a whopping 14.7 percent increase from June of 2004.

According to the OFHEO, eight states saw an increase in house value of more than 20 percent from 2004 to 2005. (See Figure 1.4 for the appreciation of all 50 states and the District of Columbia.) In other words, if you purchased a house in one of these states for $200,000, you made $40,000 while you were sleeping! For many people, that's an annual salary. If you bought that house a year ago and put 10 percent down, or $20,000, that's a 200 percent return! No one is saying that this occurrence is normal and happens every year, but it happens periodically. This inflation appreciation, then, is one cannon in your wealth-building arsenal.

If you're curious about the hottest metropolitan markets, see Figure 1.5. Some areas, like Naples, Bakersfield, Reno, Stockton, and Phoenix saw house prices jump by more than 30 percent in just one year. If you want to go "bottom fishing" (as they say in the stock-buying business), see Figure 1.6, which shows the bottom 20 markets, with annual appreciations of 3.75 percent or less. Even in these areas, properties have appreciated 10 percent to 28 percent over a 5-year period. For a listing of appreciation rates of all major and minor market areas, as compiled by the OFHEO, see the Appendix.

Suffice it to say, if you hold a property for several years, the value is going to go up. Are there exceptions? Of course. But the exceptions are rare and local economy induced. Take a look again at the average and median house prices over the past 30 years in Figure 1.1, and the trend of those prices in Figures 1.2 and 1.3. Can you comfortably predict the way those prices will go in the next ten years?

FIGURE 1.4 *House Price Appreciation by State*

House Price Appreciation by State
Percent Change in House Prices
Period Ended June 30, 2005

State	*1-Yr.	1-Yr.	Qtr.	5-Yr.	Since 1980
Nevada, (NV)	1	28.13	5.51	94.05	267.02
Arizona, (AZ)	2	27.82	9.70	66.96	235.19
Hawaii, (HI)	3	25.92	6.22	92.62	348.13
California, (CA)	4	25.16	5.26	109.68	457.62
Florida, (FL)	5	24.45	6.52	90.24	288.14
District of Columbia, (DC)	6	23.53	5.56	113.10	439.93
Maryland, (MD)	7	22.98	5.73	86.75	347.21
Virginia, (VA)	8	20.93	5.10	73.30	307.59
New Jersey, (NJ)	9	17.76	4.19	80.49	409.77
Rhode Island, (RI)	10	16.72	3.79	100.70	469.61
Delaware, (DE)	11	16.53	3.52	63.76	338.31
Oregon, (OR)	12	15.92	5.12	44.69	261.68
Washington, (WA)	13	15.84	5.29	44.96	292.26
Vermont, (VT)	14	15.76	3.47	60.16	303.12
New York, (NY)	15	14.21	2.89	71.16	492.33
Connecticut, (CT)	16	13.61	2.93	62.59	336.11
Alaska, (AK)	17	13.52	3.80	42.16	134.88
**United States ** **		**13.43**	**3.20**	**53.29**	**261.03**
Maine, (ME)	18	13.37	2.53	66.56	373.05
Pennsylvania, (PA)	19	13.01	3.22	49.59	259.51
Idaho, (ID)	20	12.92	4.14	36.56	175.47
Montana, (MT)	21	12.90	4.01	46.60	213.28
New Hampshire, (NH)	22	12.40	2.44	71.41	373.95
New Mexico, (NM)	23	11.81	4.18	35.59	174.77
Massachusetts, (MA)	24	11.80	2.30	70.70	607.07
Wyoming, (WY)	25	11.41	2.41	44.29	117.67

*Note: Ranking based on one-year appreciation.
**Note: United States figures based on weighted Census Division average.

Source: U.S. Census Bureau.

FIGURE 1.4   *House Price Appreciation by State (Continued)*

House Price Appreciation by State
Percent Change in House Prices
Period Ended June 30, 2005

State	*1-Yr.	1-Yr.	Qtr.	5-Yr.	Since 1980
Illinois, (IL)	26	9.76	2.32	40.14	240.81
Wisconsin, (WI)	27	9.47	1.97	36.41	209.44
Minnesota, (MN)	28	9.32	2.07	53.75	252.54
West Virginia, (WV)	29	9.04	2.74	32.39	124.40
North Dakota, (ND)	30	8.97	2.58	35.07	120.65
Utah, (UT)	31	8.91	3.28	21.75	185.55
South Carolina, (SC)	32	8.11	2.07	28.96	181.52
Arkansas, (AR)	33	8.03	2.21	29.25	136.04
Missouri, (MO)	34	7.71	1.61	34.10	179.32
South Dakota, (SD)	35	7.66	1.89	30.79	161.55
Alabama, (AL)	36	7.45	2.01	26.15	152.18
Tennessee, (TN)	37	6.83	2.34	24.76	171.06
Louisiana, (LA)	38	6.55	2.01	29.95	108.48
Georgia, (GA)	39	6.05	1.06	29.72	203.41
Kentucky, (KY)	40	5.92	1.41	25.12	175.80
North Carolina, (NC)	41	5.88	0.80	24.21	195.85
Iowa, (IA)	42	5.67	1.64	25.28	135.79
Colorado, (CO)	43	5.66	1.61	30.69	245.33
Nebraska, (NE)	44	5.56	1.52	22.38	146.24
Kansas, (KS)	45	5.52	1.80	26.52	130.80
Mississippi, (MS)	46	5.51	1.51	22.86	123.35
Oklahoma, (OK)	47	5.39	1.80	26.30	84.65
Michigan, (MI)	48	4.93	0.85	25.50	221.16
Ohio, (OH)	49	4.81	0.99	22.94	168.26
Indiana, (IN)	50	4.70	1.13	20.34	149.52
Texas, (TX)	51	4.68	1.75	23.37	98.76

*Note: Ranking based on one-year appreciation.
**Note: United States figures based on weighted Census Division average.

Source: U.S. Census Bureau.

FIGURE 1.5 *Top 20 Metropolitan Statistical Areas Ranked by the Highest Rates of House Price Appreciation*

*Top 20 Metropolitan Statistical Areas and Divisions With Highest Rates of House Price Appreciation
Percent Change in House Prices with MSA Rankings
Period Ended June 30, 2005

MSA	National Ranking**	1-Yr.	Qtr.	5-Yr.
Naples-Marco Island, FL	1	35.60	13.50	114.69
Bakersfield, CA	2	33.88	5.79	114.63
Merced, CA	3	32.67	8.63	131.37
Reno-Sparks, NV	4	32.27	7.29	98.45
Palm Bay-Melbourne-Titusville, FL	5	31.45	6.60	110.25
Stockton, CA	6	31.14	7.37	120.73
Phoenix-Mesa-Scottdale, AZ	7	30.48	10.90	67.31
Visalia-Porterville, CA	8	30.42	5.49	90.93
Cape Coral-Fort Myers, FL	9	29.84	9.82	106.99
Modesto, CA	10	29.56	8.09	132.29
Sarasota-Bradenton-Venice, FL	11	29.50	6.96	100.77
Punta Gorda, FL	12	29.39	7.80	109.63
Yuba City, CA	13	29.09	7.34	131.86
Coeur d'Alene, ID	14	28.98	8.12	59.90
West Palm Beach-Boca Raton-Boynton Beach, FL (MSAD)	15	28.83	6.68	113.92
Prescott, AZ	16	28.63	10.14	70.57
St. George, UT	17	28.34	10.17	47.66
Port St. Lucie-Fort Pierce, FL	18	27.20	7.12	120.98
Fresno, CA	19	27.01	5.94	123.60
Fort Lauderdale-Pompano Beach-Deerfield Beach, FL (MSAD)	20	26.93	6.87	115.85

*For composition of metropolitan statistical areas and divisions see http://www.census.gov/population/estimates/metro-city/0312msa.txt or see OFHEO HPI FAQ #8 for more information.
**Note: Rankings based on annual percentage change, for all MSAs containing at least 15,000 transactions over the last 10 years.

Source: U.S. Census Bureau.

FIGURE 1.6   *Bottom 20 Metropolitan Statistical Areas Ranked by the Lowest Rates of House Price Appreciation*

*Bottom 20 Metropolitan Statistical Areas and Divisions With Lowest Rates of House Price Appreciation
Percent Change in House Prices with MSA Rankings
Period Ended June 30, 2005

MSA	National Ranking**	1-Yr.	Qtr.	5-Yr.
Charlotte-Gastonia-Concord, NC-SC	246	3.75	0.35	18.22
Fort Worth-Arlington, TX (MSAD)	247	3.61	1.29	21.31
Tulsa, OK	248	3.44	1.46	22.04
Detroit-Livonia-Dearborn, MI (MSAD)	249	3.41	0.48	24.43
Dallas-Plano-Irving, TX (MSAD)	250	3.40	1.24	21.36
Macon, GA	251	3.29	0.55	21.71
Burlington, NC	252	3.28	0.06	16.48
Greensboro-High Point, NC	253	3.17	-0.52	17.23
Canton-Massillon, OH	254	2.83	0.60	20.52
Saginaw-Saginaw Township North, MI	255	2.82	-1.47	21.73
Anderson, SC	256	2.69	-0.82	20.44
Michigan City-La Porte, IN	257	2.67	-0.84	24.53
Spartanburg, SC	258	2.67	-1.08	16.35
Battle Creek, MI	259	2.53	-1.71	24.46
Wichita, KS	260	2.50	0.96	20.64
Hickory-Lenoir-Morganton, NC	261	2.21	0.32	18.96
Greeley, CO	262	1.88	-0.01	28.75
Kokomo, IN	263	1.08	0.29	14.65
Lafayette, IN	264	0.91	-1.10	10.88
Mansfield, OH	265	0.44	-2.73	21.01

*For composition of metropolitan statistical areas and divisions see
http://www.census.gov/population/estimates/metro-city/0312msa.txt or see OFHEO HPI FAQ
#8 for more information.
**Note: Rankings based on annual percentage change, for all MSAs containing at least 15,000
transactions over the last 10 years.

Source: U.S. Census Bureau.

Demand Appreciation

Have you ever noticed a "hot" area of town, where real estate prices are jumping even though prices in other parts of town are fairly stable? Why is that? We have the same national economy and the same local economy for both areas. How can they be different in price movement? The answer, of course, is that the hot area is experiencing demand inflation. That is, the demand for housing in that area exceeds the supply, forcing prices up.

If you've ever lived downtown in a major city, you know that the yuppies who work downtown want to live downtown for two reasons: (1) They want a short commute to work, and (2) they want to be close to the entertainment—clubs, bars, restaurants, and other nightlife spots. These urban professionals don't *want* to live downtown, they *have* to live downtown! It's not "cool" to live in the suburbs. The problem is, not enough properties are available for all the young professionals who work downtown and want to live downtown.

Have you also noticed that oceanfront or lakefront properties seem to appreciate pretty well? In many places in Florida and California, there's simply no more room to build waterfront condos or houses. About five years ago I had a broker looking for a beach condo for me in New Smyrna Beach, Florida. Many people probably have never heard of it. It's just south of Daytona Beach. New Smyrna is where the locals visit. I've been going there since I was in high school. It's a quiet, clean beach with a wide, flat beach area (great for throwing the Frisbee or playing other beach games). You don't get the sunsets like the west coast of Florida, but it's my favorite beach in the state.

My broker found a great two-bedroom, two-bath unit right on the ocean. I mean *right* on the ocean! The views from the balcony and the master bedroom were breathtaking. It was one of only 16 units on the "bulkhead," which sits just behind the seawall. It recently had been professionally upgraded and decorated. It was perhaps the best unit in one of the nicest complexes on the "no drive" part of New Smyrna Beach. I loved it and immediately put in an offer. According to the comparables, I figured it was worth about $275,000. Because I knew this was the best unit for the money on the beach, I didn't try to steal it. On this beach, in this complex, there were no steals. So I offered $264,000. I knew I could get it between $264,000 and $275,000. Problem was, it wasn't officially on the market. My broker knew the owner and that the owner was thinking of selling it. However, the owner's father was using the condo during the winter months and didn't want the family to sell it. So I put in the offer, but Granddad prevailed. The family never considered my offer.

In early 2005 I couldn't find any quads or triplexes in Orlando that interested me, so I again started looking at beach condos. After all, that's income property as well, right? The on-site management company rents it out, and you just tell them the weeks that you want it. So I went back and looked at my favorite complex. There were three units for sale in the complex—one in that bulkhead area, one ground-floor ocean-view unit overlooking the pool and ocean, and one second-story unit with a less desirable view.

The bulkhead unit wasn't nearly as nice as the unit I saw years earlier, but I was shocked at the price—$575,000. Looking at the comps, I realized that, in fact, this was a good price. It was listed by a broker whose wife I knew. He told me that, yes, the condos on this beach were appreciating at a staggering 25 percent a year. I cringed, knowing that I could have bought a much better unit for only $275,000. That is, of course, if the unit I wanted to buy five years earlier had been for sale. In short, I brought demand, but there was no supply.

I looked at the other two units, still feeling a little sick to my stomach because I missed out on some $300,000 in equity I could have acquired on the bulkhead unit I saw years earlier. I ended up buying the ground-floor unit that overlooked the pool and ocean. It didn't have quite the view as the bulkhead unit did, but it was a ground-floor unit, had a private walkway to the pool area and a gazebo, and I paid only $392,000. Knowing the beach lifestyle fairly well, I know that ground-floor units are the most desirable (try carrying beach chairs, bags, bocci balls, drinks, and other beach items up and down stairs twice a day), and this unit is one of the best-renting units in the complex (you can see it at *http://www.vrbo.com/80503*). What's more, this unit will appreciate at that same 25 percent level for some time.

While the appreciation at this time seems unusually high, I know that no more condos can be built on this beach. There's simply no more land available. And this beach is *the* place that Orlando residents love. So while the population of Orlando continues to grow (the demand), the number of beach condos (the supply) does not. I feel pretty comfortable that my long-term appreciation will do just fine.

Demand appreciation is simple—the demand for an area exceeds the supply. If you know your market area well, you know what parts of town will afford you that demand.

Forced Appreciation

But what if inflation is low and you don't see any "hot" areas? Can you still get good appreciation? Yes, by "forcing" it. You force appreciation by improving the property and increasing the rents. It's a simple formula used by most real estate investors. Let's say you have a triplex in mind that you can buy for $200,000. All three units are one-bedroom units and rent for $650 per unit. You know that the going rent for a one-bedroom unit in the area is $750. The reason the rents for your triplex are low is because the owner is absentee and doesn't take care of the place; these are long-term tenants whose rents have not been adjusted to the market; or the owner simply doesn't know the market. In most instances, rents are low because the place needs sprucing up—all the units need painting, maybe a new appliance here or there, perhaps new carpet in a unit, and so on.

Investors in income real estate properties value their acquisitions based on a number of factors, but the gross rent multiple (GRM) is perhaps the most important one for buyers of duplexes, triplexes, and quads. The GRM is a calculation an investor makes on each property to determine the relationship between the annual gross rents and the purchase price. In other words, the GRM reveals the value of the property as a multiple of its annual rents. The lower the GRM, the better the investor's bargain.

In the previous example, the GRM is 8.55 ($1,950 × 12 = $23,400 × 8.55 = $200,070). Now let's say you purchase the building, spruce it up, and increase the rents to $750 per unit, or $2,250 total per month. Annualized, that's $27,000 in rents. Multiply that by 8.55 and the new value is $230,850. By increasing the rent of each unit just $100, you have "forced" the property to appreciate by more than $30,000 (in however long it took you to clean up the units and increase the rents or change tenants).

Now let's do a little advanced real estate investing. Say you've done your homework on comparable sales of income properties and see that the going rate for the GRM is ten. Your triplex was sold for an 8.5 GRM for any number of reasons (i.e., motivated seller, unknowledgeable seller, messy property, etc.). Once you clean it up a bit and increase the rents, you could sell it at the current market rate of the 10 GRM. Here's the math:

$$\begin{array}{r} \$27,000 \quad \text{annual rents} \\ \underline{\times 10 \quad \text{GRM}} \\ \$270,000 \end{array}$$

By knowing your market, cleaning up the property, and increasing rents, you have forced your property to appreciate $70,000. Because leases are rarely over one year in length, you should have made this happen in 12 months or less. And this has nothing to do with inflation or demand. It has everything to do with market knowledge and "sweat equity."

What Happens When All Three Are Working Together?

In February of 2004 I bought a quad in a downtown Orlando area called Thornton Park. This area is a yuppieville if ever there was one. You can ride a bike to your downtown office and walk to all the "cool" restaurants and shops. Not only is it close to downtown, but it has the quaint charm of brick streets, large oaks (a lot fewer since Hurricane Charlie gave the trees a nice haircut!), and houses built in the 1920s. If you're single or a young couple, this is the "place to be."

I was looking for a quad to buy, but not necessarily in this area, since I knew the prices would be very high. However, I had my broker on a "watch" for new multiple listing service (MLS) listings. He put me on an automated e-mail that sent me listings of multifamily properties when they hit the market. One day I saw this quad for sale in Thornton Park. Because no other quads were for sale anywhere downtown, much less in the best part, I had my broker call on it within 30 minutes of it hitting the listing service. I visited it first thing in the morning the next day, along with several other investors who also saw the listing. I put in an offer the following day and ended up buying it. At the time, I felt like I bought it at the top of the market—$390,000. Normally, if you want to make money in the short term, you don't buy at the top of the market or overpay for a property. However, I know my market well and knew that demand appreciation alone would make this property a gold mine. It was also in the center of my bull's-eye for forcing appreciation.

At the time of purchase, all four units were rented. A two-bedroom, one-bath unit was leased for $595, a one-bedroom unit was rented for $675 (this unit had a fireplace, its own washer/dryer, and a private drive), another one-bedroom unit was leased for $600, and a small one-bedroom unit was leased for $525. All together, the building was generating $2,395 in monthly rents, or $28,740 a year. At the purchase price of $390,000, this property had a GRM of 13.57. In most places, that's a very high GRM. Some multiunit investors suggest not going over 7.5 for a GRM. However, I knew we were not talking about real estate theory or national averages. This was Thornton Park, the hottest part of Orlando. Besides, prior comparable sales were in the same range. So, while I knew I would be buying at the top of the market, I also knew the market would be going up, and this was a quad, the *only* quad on the market, in the best location in Thornton Park.

The seller was asking $395,000, and I initially offered $374,000. I really wanted it, but I wanted to get a feel for the seller's motivation. The seller countered at $390,000. Before I sent in a counteroffer, I found out that the seller's agent showed the property six times that day. It was a hot property, in a hot area, and someone would pay full price, if not more. I had to think about the market and the history of Thornton Park, and its future. I remembered a mistake I made in Thornton Park back in 1989.

When I was a young lawyer working downtown, I wanted to buy a house downtown to avoid the time-consuming drive in each morning. I was interested in two properties. One property was a very nice-looking two-story New Orleans–style house on a tree-lined brick street in downtown Orlando. It was 1,700 square feet, but only had two bedrooms (each was essentially a master bedroom). It had a great balcony overlooking the street and a huge attached garage. It just needed some light updating in fixtures. And you couldn't beat the location—I could *walk* to my office in five minutes!

The other property was a huge house, probably 3,500 square feet, on the corner of a busy, somewhat commercial area of a rundown neighborhood a few blocks away. The house was painted a nasty lime green color and needed a ton of work. I had worked in construction many summers growing up, so the work didn't scare me—the time and money did. I knew that I would be working long hours at the law firm and would have little time to work on, or supervise, rehabbing this house. Because I was paying off student loans for both college and law school, I also didn't have a lot of spare money to pour into a major rehab project.

In addition, I didn't like the area at all. A 7-Eleven convenience store was across the street (where a number of vagrants would hang out), a pool hall/bar was a few houses down, and a Laundromat was a few houses away. It was a noisy area with questionable neighbors. I knew that the area was "up and coming," but I didn't want the hassle or headache at this point in my life. Rather than making a decision based on real estate vision, I made it based on my personal comfort and career. I envisioned being kept up by noise early in the morning when I had a major deal going on at the law firm the next day. I bought the nice two-bedroom house for $92,000. The project I passed on? Oh, that house was *listed* for $70,000 in an area called . . . Thornton Park. To this day, I cringe every time I pass by that house. It has been rehabbed, of course, and is now used commercially. It sits on the corner of the most commercially desirable, busiest intersection in Thornton Park. It is easily worth $1.5 million. I vowed never to make that mistake again.

So when I heard about the activity on the quad that I was now looking at in Thornton Park, I just accepted the seller's counter of $390,000. I now had a vision for the area. I knew that the property would benefit from demand appreciation, and that I could force some appreciation by doing cosmetic rehab. So I bought it with a plan in mind.

All the original tenants moved out within a year. The first unit to open was the nicest unit, the one renting for $675. I decided to move into this unit so I could rehab it, and the outside of the property, as was convenient for me. Because I would live in the quad, I also could file for a homestead exemption, which would lower my property taxes.

As each tenant moved out, I went in and rehabbed the unit. For the two-bedroom, I painted it, painted the kitchen cabinets white, changed the dull knobs to brass fixtures, and installed a new stove. I increased the rent from $595 to $850. For the other one-bedroom units, I just painted and added some new vinyl flooring in one of the kitchens.

My unit's new market rent was $800. The other units were adjusted from $600 to $750, and from $525 to $575. In less than a year I had raised rents from $2,395 to $2,975. I knew that, based on my new rents, I had forced up the value. Applying a GRM of 13.57 (the going rate at the time of my purchase) to my new rents, I had a new value of $484,449 ($2,975 × 12 = $35,700 × 13.57). I had forced up the value about $94,000 in less than a year!

I also knew that the national real estate market was doing very well because of low interest rates, and that the demand for Thornton Park was growing quickly. I could sense a "perfect storm" brewing for this property—inflation appreciation, demand appreciation, and forced appreciation. After owning it a year I decided to refinance the property to pull out some equity so I could buy another property. The appraisal came in at $520,000. In just one year, I had built $130,000 in equity in this property. My guess is that about $94,000 of that equity came from forced appreciation, while the remaining $36,000 came from demand and inflation appreciation.

In December 2005, I had it appraised again at $615,000. That figure probably looks good because it reveals $225,000 in equity over 22 months. However, I know that figure is low because there have been no sales of comparables (other multiunit quads sold in Thornton Park) within the last six months. This means that the appraiser had to go outside of the area to find sales comps that he could use. Needless to say, the comps sold for much lower prices, which decreased the sales approach appraisal value. In addition, the going GRM rates outside of Thornton Park were in the range of 13 to 16. In November 2005, the GRM of listed duplexes, triplexes, and quads inside Thornton Park ranged from 18 to 22. However, until these sales are "on the books" as sold properties, the appraisers cannot use them.

At the time of this writing, I'm 23 months into the property. The national and Florida markets have remained strong (notwithstanding the bearish prognosticators), and the demand for Thornton Park has exploded. The going (asking) GRM for Thornton Park has jumped from 13.5 (when I bought in early 2004) to more than 20. With my current annual rents of $38,700 and a GRM of 20, the value of the property is now $774,000. That's an equity jump of $384,000 in 23 months! Time to sell, right? Maybe. But there are currently two duplexes and another quad on the market in Thornton Park, all less desirable than my property, and in poorer locations, listed for GRMs of 25, 25, and 33.3, respectively. Because I know that every lender's appraiser is going to look for comparable sales, I want to see what these sell for and get them "on the books." The quad is listed for a GRM of 33.3. If it sells for a GRM of 27, let's say, I know my property will command at least that. My rents are about to go up again also, to $3,375. If I get a GRM of just 25 at that level, my new value, supported by comparable sales, would be $1,012,500. That would be an equity gain of $622,500 in two years.

Frankly, I think a GRM of over 20 is crazy, and I don't think those other properties will sell for GRMs of over 22. However, real estate is a funny thing, especially in hot areas. In December 2005, I bought a triplex on the outskirts of downtown Orlando for a 16.5 GRM (the lowest listed GRM for any multifamily property in that zip code). It's in a marginal area and is a bit dumpy. So I know that anything in Thornton Park has to pull a GRM of 18 or higher. But, until other multifamily properties sell in Thornton Park, I can't know for sure what mine is worth. I do know this: it's worth somewhere between $615,000 and $1,012,500. As such, I've created equity of between $225,000 and $622,500 in just two years.

Remember that the GRM is just one valuation method. Another valuation method that appraisers use is "comparable sales." This method is not quite as reliable for evaluating income properties, so it is a secondary valuation method. Using this method, properties can be compared using sale prices on a price-per-square-foot basis. Because a house two doors down from mine just sold for $305 per square foot, this valuation method would render a similar result as the income approach.

Let's do the math. My quad has 3,122 heated square feet: 3,122 × $305 = $952,210. Using that valuation method, I had an equity increase, or a real net worth increase, of $562,000 ($952,000 – $390,000). Technically, I should also add the appreciation of my beach condo to my equity or net worth gain because I used some of the $48,000 refinance money to buy that property. Based on a recent sale, I have another $38,000 from appreciation of the condo.

In 23 months, then, I have somewhere between $263,000 and 660,500 in equity or net worth gain initiated from this one transaction. Did I mention that I started this process with no money down? I also bought the triplex with some of the $48,000 that I pulled out of property #1, but it's too complicated to try to factor that in as well. I think you see the point.

Granted, this kind of appreciation is unusual, but it does reflect what can happen when you have all three aspects of appreciation working for you. At the very least, you know you can always force appreciation. If demand or inflation appreciation comes along, so much the better.

TAX BENEFITS

Sale of Personal Residence

Did I mention that if I sold this quad, the first $250,000 in gain would be tax-free? When you live in a residential property for two years, the IRS allows a single person to take the first $250,000 gain tax-free, or a married couple to take the first $500,000 tax-free. Even though this is a multifamily, income-producing property, it is classified as residential because it is under five units. I need to wait to sell this property for just another month and I can utilize this IRS tax windfall.

1031 Exchange

As an alternative, I could sell it now and use a different tax benefit called a 1031 exchange. If I roll all the gain into another "like-kind" property, meaning an income property, I can delay the taxes indefinitely into the future. More on the 1031 exchange in Chapter 13.

Interest Deduction

Here's a benefit every homeowner knows. At the beginning of every year, your mortgage company will send you an IRS Form 1098, showing how much interest you paid on your mortgage (for your personal residence) for the prior year. The lender sends this information to you so that you can deduct the interest you paid for the prior year. If you are not living in the property, you'll want to depreciate the building.

Depreciation

If you own an income-producing residential property (which is all this book will cover), you can depreciate your building (not the value of the land) over 27.5 years. Let's say your property is worth $200,000. You check with your property appraiser (many will have a Web site) to see how your land is valued compared to the building itself. For example, your land may be given a value of $40,000, while the building is assessed at $160,000. You can then take this amount and divide it by 27.5 to obtain your annual deduction. Your deduction calculation would look like this:

$160,000   building assessment
÷ 27.5   depreciation allowance
$5,818.18   amount you can deduct annually

Keep two other things in mind with depreciation. First, you also can depreciate your personal property in the building. For example, carpeting, drapes, fixtures, and appliances are all things that "depreciate" or wear out over time. As such, you can include them in your depreciation building total. Second, if you sell the property, you must "recapture" this deduction. This means you must add any deductions taken to your overall gain. Many people avoid this problem by refinancing their property, rather than selling it, or using a 1031 Exchange to protect their gain.

Repairs and Improvements

For rental properties, any repairs you make are 100 percent tax deductible in the year you make them. If you make an *improvement,* you deduct that cost over 27.5 years. Let's say you spend $7,500 to fix up your property. If you classify that work as a repair, that's an immediate $7,500 deduction. If you classify it as an improvement, then you have an annual deduction of $272.73 for 27.5 years. More than likely, you'd prefer to classify your work as a repair rather than as a deduction. But what makes it a repair versus an improvement?

Sandy Botkin, certified public accountant and author of *Reduce Your Taxes—Big Time,* states that a repair is work that keeps a property in ordinary, efficient operating condition. An improvement, on the other hand, makes the property better in some aspect. For example, an improvement would

- increase the value of the property,
- make the property last longer, or
- adapt the property to a new or different use.

Write-off of Losses

If you actively manage your investment property (i.e., selecting new tenants, showing the property, collecting rents, etc.), you can write off, or deduct, up to $25,000 of your real estate losses against your other (i.e., W-2) income, subject to certain income limitations. If you are single or file jointly with your spouse, you can use 100 percent of the deduction if your adjusted gross income is $100,000 or less ($50,000 if married but filing separately). If your income exceeds $100,000, you lose $1 in deduction for every $2 that your income exceeds the $100,000 threshold.

Because tax benefits are real benefits that affect what you put in your pocket, factor these numbers in when analyzing a property, either for purchase or sale, or reducing your taxable income. Refer to your accountant or tax advisor for applying these IRS rules to your property.

EQUITY BUILDUP

This benefit is also called "reduction of principal." Unless you have an interest-only loan, your mortgage payment will include both interest and principal. If you have a "fully amortized" loan, paying principal and interest, you will own your property free and clear at the end of your mortgage term (assuming that you did not further encumber the property).

Assume that you bought a property for $200,000 and put 10 percent down. Your mortgage payment would be calculated on a $180,000 principal loan. At 6.5 percent interest, for example, amortized over 30 years, your mortgage payment would be $1,137.72. Assume that you have tenants that cover your mortgage payment. At the end of one year, your tenants would have paid 100 percent of your payments, and also paid down the principal of your mortgage by $2,011.90. At the end of 10 years, your tenants would have paid down your mortgage by $27,402.90. This equity buildup works like a secret piggy bank—each month your tenants make a small deposit to your account. Eventually, they will pay off your mortgage for you and you will own the property free and clear.

LEVERAGE

People become rich in real estate from leverage. Yes, you can make good money or shelter income from the other benefits, but leverage is what builds real wealth. This factor is so important to your long-term wealth-building plan that I've dedicated an entire chapter to it (see Chapter 3). For now, let's just give one simple example of how leverage works, and why it is important for you to use.

Assume that you desire to purchase a $200,000 duplex. If you had the money, you could pay for it in cash. You would now own it free and clear. Now assume that the house appreciates 10 percent because of inflation and demand. Your house is now worth $220,000. But your rate of return is only 10 percent. Now suppose that you put down only 20 percent on the property, or $40,000. Your rate of return has jumped to 50 percent (you made $20,000 on a $40,000 investment). And if you put only 10 percent down? One hundred percent. Five percent down? Two hundred percent.

Can you see the importance of your return on investment (ROI)? In the first example, you made $20,000 on your $200,000 investment. What if you took that $200,000 and bought 10 houses with 10 percent down? How much would you make? Let's compare:

No Leverage: Cash purchase of one house

$$\begin{array}{rl} \$200,000 & \text{cash purchase of \$200,000 asset} \\ \underline{\times\,0.10} & \text{appreciation} \\ \$20,000 & \text{gain} \end{array}$$

10 Times Leverage: Purchase of 10 houses with 10 percent down

$$\begin{array}{rl} \$2,000,000 & \text{Value of 10 houses @ \$200,000 each} \\ \underline{\times\,0.10} & \text{appreciation} \\ \$200,000 & \text{gain} \end{array}$$

By understanding leverage, you have increased your gain, or net worth, by $180,000 over the cash purchase scenario. Can you see how this leverage will change your life over 20 years? This is why there is no better investment for most people than real estate. But there are hundreds, if not thousands, of books on real estate investing. Which type of real estate, and what type of strategy, is best for the new investor? Which type is best for you?

In the next chapter, I'll show why investing in residential multifamily real estate is the best form of real estate investing, especially for beginners. I'll then go into detail on why leverage is so important for real wealth building, and how to use it safely over the long term. I've learned a few "tricks of the trade" to increase your profits (or decrease your down payment) over the years, and I'll explain them in Chapter 4. I'll then explain whether it is best to "buy and hold," "pyramid," or refinance.

Part II of the book will deal with all aspects of buying a property, including finding, analyzing, and financing it. Part III will cover selling your property, and the tax implications of doing so. Finally, Part IV of the book will lay out different plans for you to follow for starting your wealth-building program. Some people have money but little time. Others have time but little money. Still others may have made some financial mistakes in the past but don't have 30, or perhaps even 20, years to make something happen to secure their financial future. My goal is to give each person a safe, workable plan to secure their financial future (not to mention peace of mind) for themselves and their families. This plan has worked for me, and I know it will work for you, too.

2

WHY RESIDENTIAL
MULTIFAMILY IS THE BEST

Now, one thing I tell everyone is learn about real estate.
Repeat after me: Real estate provides the highest returns, the greatest values and the least risk.

—Armstrong Williams, Capital Community News

Over the years, I have invested in almost every type of real estate and used almost every type of strategy—single-family homes, multifamily, vacant land, flips, lease options, foreclosures, wrap mortgages, tax deed properties, and tax liens. I can tell you that they *all* work. Yes, you can make money and nice profits with every type of real estate or strategy. But before choosing a real estate investment type or strategy, every investor needs to ask these questions:

1. How lucrative is it?
2. How safe is it?
3. How simple is it?
4. How easy is it to finance?
5. How much time does it take?
6. What best suits my restrictions, talents, and resources?
7. Am I comfortable doing this?

Every type of real estate investing has pros and cons, including investing in residential real estate. In fact, every type of *investment* has pros and cons. For example, some people don't like investing in real estate because they don't want to deal with tenants. Those folks may want to look only at flipping, or investing in tax liens (safe, priority liens secured by real estate). You may be a commercial real estate broker with a particular expertise in commercial properties. Most likely, you'd want to invest in that type of property. You may want to develop property by buying raw land (or speculating for a future sale). If that's you, you may want to look at how to acquire raw land cheaply, such as through tax deed sales, foreclosures, and auctions.

Everyone has different resources, talents, temperaments, and goals. Find what works for you. Following is a list of what I believe are the best books for different types of real estate investing:

- **General real estate investing:** Milt Tanzer, *Real Estate Investments and How to Make Them* (Prentice Hall, 1996); and Martin Stone and Spencer Strauss, *The Unofficial Guide to Real Estate Investing* (IDG Books Worldwide, 1999).
- **Buy-and-hold strategy:** David Schumacher, *Buy and Hold* (Schumacher Enterprises, 2004).
- **Single-family, rehab and flip:** Kevin Myers, *Buy It, Fix It, Sell It, Profit!* 2d ed. (Dearborn Trade Publishing, 2003).
- **Single-family, low-end ("ugly houses"), rehab and hold:** Jay Decima, *Start Small, Profit Big in Real Estate* (McGraw-Hill, 2005).
- **Tax-deed acquisitions (or tax-lien purchases):** Larry Loftis, *Profit by Investing in Real Estate Tax Liens* (Dearborn Trade Publishing, 2005).
- **Tenant management:** Leigh Robinson, *Landlording* (Express, 1999, Eighth Edition). This is not a strategy per se, but if you have tenants, this is *the* book to read.

- **Commercial multifamily (apartments, five units and up):** Steve Berges, *Buying and Selling Apartment Buildings* (Wiley, 2005).
- **Residential multifamily (2–4 units):** You have it in your hands.

Now that I have given you what I believe are the best books on different types of investing, or strategies, let me pick them apart (mine included)! In my experience, investing in residential multifamily properties provides the most benefits of real estate investing, with the least disadvantages, but you be the judge after reading this chapter.

The focus of this book is investing in "residential multifamily" properties. Given this, it is important to understand the difference between *residential* and *commercial*. Many real estate agents and investors do not know the difference between the two.

"Residential" means one to four units.
"Residential multifamily" means two to four units.
"Commercial multifamily" means five units or more.

The reason this is significant is because financing a residential property is far easier than financing a commercial property. When you move from a four-unit building to a five-unit building, everything changes. I'll discuss financing later in the book, but now let's look at how investing in residential multifamily properties differs from other methods of real estate investing.

OTHER TYPES OF REAL ESTATE INVESTING

Buying and Renting Single-Family Homes

Most people are very familiar with this type of investing. You simply buy a house, rent it out, and let inflation and equity buildup (and perhaps forced appreciation, if you rehabbed it) do their work. This program works and is fairly easy to do and finance. Here is why multifamily investing is better:

Vacancies. If you rent out a house and you have a vacancy, how much vacancy do you have? One hundred percent, right? Who covers the mortgage and other expenses during this vacancy? You do. And the mortgage payment on the house where you live doesn't go away, either. With two mortgage payments (and utilities, taxes, insurance, and yard maintenance), if you don't rent that house out very quickly, you'll soon become a "motivated" seller! If you own a quad and have a vacancy, what is your overall vacancy rate? Twenty-five percent, right? Who covers your expenses during this vacancy? Your other tenants. If you purchased the property right, and your rents are in the right place, your other three tenants should cover your expenses, or be very close to covering them.

Economies of scale. You may have learned this concept in your economics class. It has to do with efficiency. Let's say you own three houses. Managing three houses, in three different locations, is much more work and expense than managing a triplex. This is why institutional investors, like real estate investment trusts (REITS), will own one apartment complex of 400 units rather than 20 complexes of 20 units each.

Competition. For every middle- to low-range single-family house for sale, you have three groups of potential buyers: live-in owners, investors who want to rent it, and investors who want to flip it. For multifamily properties, typically you have only investors looking at them. In addition, because you rarely have foreclosures and flips for multifamily properties, *fewer* investors are looking at them. Because of these two factors, your competition for multi-family properties is much less than with single-family homes.

Time. To have three sets of rent checks coming in from houses, you have to find three properties, negotiate the purchase of three properties, perform due diligence (i.e., conduct inspec-tions, obtain rent and sales comparables, etc.) three times, and so on. You have to do this when you buy and sell. It just takes less time doing this on one property (like a triplex) versus doing it for three.

Rent. Your "rent-to-cost" ratio is better with multiunit proper-ties. For example, if you buy a $200,000 house, you may not be able to rent it for more than $1,000 per month. Assuming that you put 10 percent down, your mortgage payment (at 6 percent interest amortized over 30 years) is $1,079. You have negative cash flow and you haven't even factored in taxes, insurance, or mainte-nance. If you bought a triplex for $200,000, on the other hand, you should be able to rent each unit out for at least $500, or $1,500 total. Your expenses are covered.

Pets. Pets damage properties. Cats and dogs can leave a house with a very ugly smell (use your imagination), as well as lots of fleas. In addition, dogs dig up backyards, ruin landscaping, bark, and sometimes bite people. Male cats sometimes "spray" their territory, or where a female cat is likely to travel. If you have a house, tenants expect the right to own a pet. In an apartment unit, however, most tenants don't automatically expect to have pet privileges. I don't normally allow pets in my rental units, and I don't have problems with fleas, barking dogs, funny odors, or in-creased liability.

Distasteful environment. If you want decent positive cash flow from the date of purchase, you'll need to buy in the lower end of the house market, in most instances. In other words, you need to buy cheap houses to make the numbers work. As a general rule, the worse the neighborhood, the better the cash flow (and the lower the appreciation).

You can buy residential multifamily properties in this market, too, if you want to. But the numbers will work fine buying in middle-class neighborhoods, and even in some upper middle-class areas. Make no mistake, though, you can receive terrific cash flow in these lower-class areas. You just have to be able to stomach the lifestyle and problems created by tenants in these types of properties. I'd just as soon work in areas that don't ruin my day, or my lunch.

"Flipping" Single-Family Homes

Many people engage in flipping houses, which entails buying a property and quickly reselling it for a profit, on a full- or part-time basis, and many books are written on the subject. It can be very lucrative, especially if you have a system in place to mass-market for cheap houses. You've probably seen a number of signs like "We Buy Ugly Houses." I know at least three companies that do this nationally. Countless investors also flip homes on their own, or with a partner or family member, in every community. Here is why investing in residential multifamily properties is preferable:

Need for considerable cash. Flipping is very popular and the competition is fierce. Most people who sell their properties quickly to these types of companies need to get out of a financial jam. As such, most flippers offer all cash in just a few days. Without the need for a lender, they don't need to wait the typical 30 days to close. That means these buyers can fork up $50,000 to

$150,000 in a few days. How many normal folks can do that? What's more, this type of investing is really all about marketing to people who need cash quickly. I know a guy who is a partner in one of these companies who told me that his was a "marketing" company. He told me that the product could be anything, because the marketing produces the inventory and the profits. That's why his company spends $20,000 or more *each month* in billboard advertising. Want to compete with that?

Competition. See the previous paragraph.

Risk of not selling quickly. I once bought a house in Memphis. It was a great house—a four-bedroom, two bath, with hardwood floors, in a great area. A dentist owned it and had moved on to a nicer, bigger house. He was motivated because he now had a vacant house on his hands and was paying two mortgage payments (and other expenses). He had three appraisals that he gave to me: one for $187,000 (this one was from about a year earlier), one for $200,000, and one for $215,000. The latter two were recent and suggested to me that the property was worth between $200,000 to $215,000. He sold it to me for $150,000. On paper I had equity of between $50,000 to $65,000. Sweet.

I had some light cosmetic work done and immediately put it on the market for $185,000. No bites. I waited a couple of months. No offers. I was shocked. The property was on a busy street but it was a beautiful house in a great neighborhood with lots of huge, mature trees. To this day, I don't know what the problem was. It just didn't sell. After having this property on the market for about three months, *I* became the motivated seller! I dropped the price to $180,000. Still no offers.

In desperation, I rented the house out at just enough to cover my expenses. This occurred in about the fourth month. I ended up selling it a year later for $180,000. But it taught me two lessons. First, you can't rely on what an appraisal says. Second, it taught me the risk of flipping properties—holding costs. Like Robert Kiyosaki says, "On every deal I either make money or get experience." I learned this disadvantage from experience.

Need for rehab skills or time. People who flip properties actually fall into two categories. The big companies, the ones that use billboards, typically are "wholesalers." They find properties that they can acquire for $0.30 to $0.60 on the dollar and just immediately sell them to "retailers" for $0.60 to $0.80 on the dollar. The "retailer" is the one who actually rehabs the house and sells it for fair market value. Most people who flip houses are buying them, either directly from a seller or from a wholesaler, for $0.50 to $0.80 on the dollar.

To make much money in that range, particularly with lower-priced homes (which is the market for flipping), many, if not most, investors are doing much of the work themselves. So how skilled are you with a hammer? A paintbrush? A power saw? And how much time do you have? If you are not very handy or don't have much extra time, stay with duplexes, triplexes, and quads.

Because multifamily properties are rarely flipped, this scenario doesn't really apply. Yes, you do want properties that need light cosmetic work, but painting is easy and you can do it as each unit is vacated. With the house-flipping scenario, most of those "need cash quick" houses require more rehab than just painting.

High transaction costs. For each house you flip, you incur closing costs and, typically, broker commissions. For closing costs, you actually get hit twice—once when you buy and once when you sell (for a breakdown of closing costs, see Chapter 11).

Let's say you bought a $100,000 house. Assume closing costs are about $3,000. Now let's add in your broker's commission when you sell the property. Commissions on residential homes generally run from 5 percent to 7 percent. Assume that you sell the house for $160,000. That's a nice $60,000 for your efforts, right? But that's not your profit. Using an average commission of 6 percent, you'd lose $9,600 off the top. Then you have to subtract the $3,000 in closing costs when buying and selling (I'll keep the costs the same for the sake of this example). So you're now out $15,600 in transaction fees.

But we're not done yet. You didn't buy it, rehab it, and sell it overnight. In most instances, you'll need to make at least two mortgage payments. Assuming a $90,000 loan (until recently, these investor flips required 20 percent down) at 6 percent interest amortized for 30 years, your mortgage payment is about $540 per month. Now add in another $40 per month for insurance, another $100 for taxes, another $100 for utilities, and another $100 for lawn maintenance—your overhead nut has reached $880.

Assume you close on January 1 and that you can rehab it in one month and get a buyer in 60 days. This means that you get a contract on March 1. It now takes another 30 days to close on April 1. Here are your carrying costs:

January 1–31:

Utilities	$100
Yard	100
Insurance	40
Taxes	100
Total monthly upkeep	$340

You won't have a mortgage payment until February 1.

February 1–28:

Mortgage payment	$540
Monthly upkeep	340
Total	$880

March 1–31:

Mortgage payment	$540
Monthly upkeep	340
Total	$880

Total carrying cost from January 1 to March 31	$2,100
Total closing costs for purchase and sale	6,000
Broker commissions	9,600
Total transaction and carrying costs	$17,700

Now let's say you incurred only $10,000 in rehab expenses because you did most of the work yourself. You now have $27,700 into the project. Subtracted from your $60,000 gross profit, your net profit on the deal was $32,300. But remember, this process took you three months to complete.

Many people could live with this scenario. But what if you couldn't sell it for six months? Now your holding costs double. Anyway you look at it, this process has risk.

Taxes. The current tax laws favor holding a property for at least one year. If you are flipping properties, you want to turn it as quickly as possible. Five months would probably be the longest you would ever be willing to hold a property in the flipping game. Unfortunately, the IRS will punish you for not holding it for at least one year. If you hold it for one year before selling, your profits will be considered "long-term capital gains" and will be taxed at only 15 percent. If you sell before one year, the IRS will consider it "ordinary income" and will tax you at your current personal tax bracket rate. In other words, you're likely to pay 33 percent in taxes, rather than the long-term tax rate of 15 percent. Consider the effect of a $50,000 pretax profit:

Flipped within one year:		Sold after one year:	
$50,000	gross profit	$50,000	gross profit
× 0.33	tax rate	× 0.15	tax rate
$16,500	tax due	$7,500	tax due
$33,500	net profit	$42,500	net profit

Clearly, the tax implications are a major drawback to flipping properties. In the hypothetical situation where the gross profit was $60,000, after subtracting holding and transaction costs, the remaining profit was only $32,300. However, that's still not the net profit because the IRS hasn't taken its bite yet. If you are in the 33 percent tax bracket, you now have to subtract another $10,793 from the $32,300, leaving you with a final net profit of only $21,507. And remember, it will take three to five months to receive that profit. Can you see how it will be very difficult to build wealth by just flipping properties?

Foreclosures

One of the most popular real estate investment strategies is foreclosures—mortgage ("bank") foreclosures. Foreclosures have disadvantages similar to those of flipping, and an additional disadvantage that is unique to foreclosures.

Thin margins because of competition. Many years ago you may have been able to pick up a property at a foreclosure auction for $0.50 on the dollar. Nowadays, however, you're likely to be in the $.60- to $.80-on-the-dollar range. Many of the people in the rehab/flip game look for their properties at foreclosure auctions. Because you still have to rehab, market, and sell the property, your profit margins are very thin.

You also may have heard of *tax deed* foreclosures. I've bought several properties this way. In my experience, most properties sold at tax deed auctions sell for around $0.50 on the dollar. That's the upside. The downside is that these properties are typically vacant lots or abandoned properties that need a ton of work. This is like a scavenger hunt where you are looking for that "diamond in the rough." If this interests you, see my book *Profit by Investing in Real Estate Tax Liens.*

All-cash buyers. When you buy at any kind of foreclosure auction, you need all cash, up front. Typically, auctions require a deposit of 10 percent down upon winning the bid, with the remaining 90 percent balance due within 24 hours. That requirement alone eliminates almost all buyers other than the professional rehab investors.

Trashed properties. Many times when someone is about to lose his or her home, he or she may trash the property—ranging from holes in the walls to missing appliances and fixtures. What's worse, oftentimes potential buyers will not be able to go inside of the house before the sale.

Preforeclosures

Probably 90 percent of general real estate seminars promote working in preforeclosures. What this means is that you market for people who are about to lose their homes, and you "rescue" them from losing their home to foreclosure. In addition to all the disadvantages to foreclosures, another disadvantage, the *biggest* disadvantage, is the moral turpitude of the general practice espoused.

On more times than I care to recount, here's basically the scenario I've heard at real estate seminars. The speaker mentions finding a person who is about to lose her property from a foreclosure. In one example I recall, an elderly lady had about $60,000 in equity in her home. Someone, likely her widower, had been making payments on the house for many years. She is about to lose her house because she can't make the $750 payments and is four months behind.

Alas, the real estate guru comes to the "rescue." He "saves" her by keeping her credit from having a foreclosure stain; he buys her house from her and gives her $2,000 cash to help her move into an apartment. So the guru investor puts up $3,000 to bring her mortgage current, plus maybe some $500 in late fees, and takes over her mortgage. He gives her $2,000 to send her on her way. He then spends about $500 to spruce up the place and sells it for fair market value, capturing her $60,000 in equity, less his acquisition costs. In short, she gets $2,000 and he gets about $54,000. What an angel.

I've heard some seminar speakers talk about how magnanimous they were by letting the former owners stay in the properties and now rent them. Keep in mind, of course, that the lady in this example couldn't make the current mortgage payments. How long will she remain a tenant?

About the only scenario that I think is morally tolerable, at best, is to split the sale proceeds with the prior owner. That way, the lady still loses the property but walks away with about half of her original equity. Personally, I don't have the stomach to do even that.

Vacation Properties

Vacation properties, whether beach or mountain homes or condos, are also income properties. I own a beautiful beach condo so I'm very familiar with the pros and cons of this type of investment. The three main benefits of owning a vacation property are personal use, professional management, and excellent appreciation.

I can use my condo any time I want by calling the management company and telling them to block (i.e., not rent) the dates I have in mind. I typically block mine for the warm, three-day holidays—Memorial Day, Independence Day, and Labor Day. I lose great rents for those times but I get to use it myself and invite family or friends. I then use it periodically on many weekends.

The professional, on-site management does all the work to generate income. They market it, secure the renters, collect the rents and deposits, schedule housekeeping, handle any repairs, and provide monthly and annual statements. It's a turnkey operation. I absolutely love this investment property.

As noted earlier, the beach condos where mine is located have been appreciating at 20 to 25 percent a year. You will be hardpressed to find many places that will consistently beat that average. As Mark Twain once said, responding to why one should invest in real estate, "They don't make land anymore." Indeed, and they especially don't make oceanfront properties anymore. Having said that, here are the disadvantages:

Negative cash flow. I bought my unit for $392,000. While I have one of the best-renting units in the building, at that price you can't expect the rents, which only come in certain months, to cover your annual overhead. Here's what typically happens for a beach condo. The Northern "snowbirds" will come down and rent the unit for January through March. April through July expect to rent the unit two to four weeks of each month. August may bring one week's rental. September and October will be dead. November may get a renter over the Thanksgiving holiday, and December may rent the last week, or the last two weeks of the month.

So I'll have nice positive cash flow for a few months, break even for a couple months, and have negative cash flow the rest of the year. At best, I'll break even for the year. Most of the time, however, I'll have a small negative cash flow (about $8,000 to $12,000 per year, not factoring in tax deductions and appreciation). Most people who own beach condos consider the family use, memories, and appreciation well worth the negative cash flow.

Unexpected expenses. Unless you are on the board of the condo association, you'll likely be surprised from time to time by assessments for upkeep or repairs. I recently received a notice from my association that said the board had just passed an assessment to repaint the railings and doorsills around the complex, to make a few repairs remaining from hurricane damage, and to take care of a few other minor upkeep items. The assessment was $541 for the next four months. Surprise! While I didn't like seeing this notice, one of the things that attracted me to this complex was how perfectly everything was maintained. It is constantly being landscaped, groomed, and painted to appear brand new. These things cost money, of course, but they increase the value of your unit.

Inability to force appreciation dramatically. Unlike other investment properties, you can't really rehab your condo unit to force appreciation dramatically. Sure, you can modernize your unit and increase the rents, but beach condos are not evaluated on the basis of the GRM. In most cases, an appraiser will only look at other sales in your complex to determine value.

ADVANTAGES TO OWNING RESIDENTIAL MULTIFAMILY PROPERTIES

Residential multifamily properties—2–4 units—are known as duplexes, triplexes, and quadraplexes ("quads" for short). In the north, you may hear them referred to as "brownstones," which refers to the reddish-brown sandstone on the building's exterior. In places such as Chicago, they are called "three flats" or "four flats." Any multifamily building with five or more units is considered "commercial" property. Here are the advantages to owning residential multifamily properties.

Easiest to finance. If you buy a commercial property and use a bank as your lender, you'll need to put 20 percent down. Because commercial properties are normally more expensive than residential properties, 20 percent down usually means you can't consider those properties. Thus, even if you have a wonderful and perfectly priced five-unit multifamily building, you'll likely pass on it when you realize what 20 percent down amounts to.

Until recently, all "investor properties" (meaning you don't live in it) required a 20 percent minimum down payment, regardless of whether the property was a single-family house or a shopping center. Now, however, lenders are allowing buyers to put less than 20 percent down by using second mortgages. For example, if you were looking at a triplex that you could buy for $200,000, until a few years ago you were required to put down $40,000. The bank had an 80 percent loan-to-value (LTV) ratio.

Lenders now are allowing some flexibility. They will not exceed their 80 percent LTV, but they will allow you to further encumber the property, because their lien is in first position. As such, you can now put down 10 percent, have the primary lender provide a first mortgage for 80 percent and have a secondary lender provide a second mortgage for the remaining 10 percent. In fact, in some cases you can even put down 5 percent and have the secondary lender take 15 percent.

This lending flexibility allows you to buy more properties and get a far better return on investment (ROI). Again, this flexibility is only for up to four units. Because the property is still considered residential, you can get a 30-year fixed mortgage, with the lowest interest rate, and no balloon. Compare the financing terms in Figure 2.1 for residential versus commercial properties.

As you can see from Figure 2.1, financing a residential property is easier, or better, in every category. In fact, most investors

FIGURE 2.1   *Financing Terms for Residential versus Commercial Properties*

Terms Available	Residential Property (1 to 4 units)	Commercial Property (5 or more units)
Down payment	0 to 10 percent	20 percent
Fixed rate?	Yes	No, pick from 3/5/7-year ARM (adjustable rate mortgage)
Maximum term	30 years	25 years
Balloon?	No	Typical
Interest rate	Lowest market rate	1 to 1.5 points above residential

will not be able to finance any commercial properties. That's fine, however, because the terms for financing a residential property, even if it is an expensive quad, are very accommodating. And you will have no problem finding a duplex, triplex, or quad to buy when you are ready.

In addition, if you plan to live in one of the units, your lender will allow you to use 75 percent of the scheduled income to offset your qualifying loan ratios. In other words, your bank will add 75 percent of your rents to your occupational (W-2 or 1099) income, as if this money came from your job.

Maximum leverage. Because you can put less down on a residential multifamily property, you will be able to use more leverage in your purchase. As a result, your ROI will be better. For example, assume that you are buying a $300,000 property and that the property nets, after all expenses, $350 per month, or $4,200 per year. If the property is commercial, you'll need to put down 20 percent, or $60,000. What is your ROI at the end of the year? If you divide $4,200 by $60,000, your cash-on-cash yield is only 7 percent. Not too exciting.

But let's now say that this is a residential multifamily property. You now can put down 10 percent, or $30,000. Your yield has doubled to a very respectable 14 percent. And what if you put down only 5 percent, or $15,000? Your yield now doubles again, to an outstanding 28 percent.

I can hear your objection, "But if I put less down, I won't have as much cash flow, which reduces my yield." This is true, but the difference in yield will be less dramatic than you think because the difference in mortgage payments will be only slight. If you put down 10 percent, your loan amount is $270,000. At 6 percent interest, amortized over 30 years, your mortgage payment (principal and interest) will be $1,618.79. At 5 percent down, with the same terms, your payment would be $1,708.72, or $89.93 more. This means that you would have a reduction in cash flow of $1,079.15 on an annual basis. Thus, your cash flow for the year would drop slightly, from $4,200 to $3,121.

My new cash-on-cash yield, with 5 percent down, is still an excellent 20.8 percent. Compare that with the 14 percent yield with 10 percent down. Just for fun, let's also compare the numbers of the commercial property with 20 percent down. Let's assume that the $350 per month cash flow was at 10 percent down, so we'll have a bit more cash flow with 20 percent down. With a $300,000 purchase price and $60,000 down, I'll have a loan of $240,000. However, my term can't be longer than 25 years, and my interest will be a bit higher, say at 6.5 percent (forget ARMs for the comparative illustration). At these terms, my payment is still $1,620.50, or even *more* than it was with 10 percent down on my residential property.

Compare all three yields, then, with the same purchase price of $300,000:

Property Type	Down	Yield
Commercial (5+ units)	20.0%	7.0%
Residential (1 to 4 units)	10.0%	14.0%
Residential (1 to 4 units)	5.0%	20.8%

Residential multifamily properties clearly provide the best opportunity to maximize your yield and make more money on your investment. Over time, the result will be dramatic.

Right price range. When you are purchasing 2–4 unit properties, the purchase price will be about the same as that for a single-family home of similar quality. In fact, many duplexes, triplexes, and quads are converted single-family homes. One way to compare the single-family house to the multifamily dwelling is to look at square feet. In most cases, a single-family home that is 2,100 square feet will cost you about the same as a triplex that is 2,100 square feet. As such, if you can afford a single-family home, you can usually afford its multifamily equivalent.

Less vacancy risk. As noted earlier, if you have a rental house and you have a vacancy, you have a vacancy rate of 100 percent. You now have two mortgage payments (and expenses) and you are getting your lunch eaten! If you have a quad and you have a vacancy, your overall vacancy is only 25 percent and you still can cover your expenses. Even with a vacancy in a triplex, you still may be able to cover your expenses. For this reason, residential multifamily properties are the safest of all real estate investments.

Right rent range. Let's return to the 2,100-square-foot home and the 2,100-square-foot triplex. For a nice quality triplex unit of 700 square feet, you may get about $800 per month in rent. That's $1.143 in rent per square foot. To get the same bang for your buck with the house, however, you'd have to rent it out for $2,400. Good luck. If your renter can afford a $2,400 rent payment, why would he or she be renting? Chances are, the house probably will command a rent of only $1,200 per month, or about half what the triplex can bring. Even if the triplex units rent for only $600 per month, that's still $600 more per month than the house. Over a year, the triplex will produce $7,200 more than the house.

By the way, which tenant do you think is easier to find—the one who pays $1,200 per month or the one who pays $600 or $800 per month? As a general rule, the cheaper the rent, the larger the tenant pool. In most cases, it will take you longer to rent the $1,200 house than the less expensive triplex units.

Easiest to improve. With a house, you have to rehab the entire house, inside and out, before you can rent it. With a multifamily property, however, you can work on each unit as that tenant leaves. That is, you can piecemeal the work. If you are doing all the work yourself, this is a significant advantage. What's more, you could move into one of the units and rehab that one in your spare time. In addition, if you lived in one of your units, you wouldn't have to drive across town just on Saturday to work on an open unit. By living there, you have easy and convenient access to work steadily throughout the week.

Economies of scale (lower management costs). As noted previously, multifamily properties will allow you to take advantage of economies of scale. Your transaction costs, management costs, and use of time and labor will be less with a concentration of units. Imagine managing four houses, in four different locations, versus managing one quad (especially if you live there).

Walk into cash flow. Seldom are single-family homes sold with tenants in them. The house is normally either vacant or the owner occupies it. Thus, when you buy it, you have zero cash flow. What you have is a hole in your pocket. That "sucking sound," as Ross Perot quipped about the North America Free Trade Agreement (NAFTA), is the noise of your money running through a siphon into that house—mortgage payment, insurance, taxes, utilities, and yard maintenance. Until you get a tenant in there, you have an uncapped siphon into your bank account.

With residential multifamily properties, they are almost always fully rented when you buy them (most sellers don't put them up for sale with a vacancy). As such, you walk into cash flow from the day you buy it. Assume you are buying a quad with four tenants paying $700 each. Where else can you walk into a residual cash flow of $2,800 per month? You don't have to worry about the risk of not meeting your mortgage payment or other expense obligations. You know from the date of closing that your expenses are covered. If you happen to have a vacancy, or get one quickly, great—now you can rehab that unit and raise the rent.

Free money at closing. In the previous quad example, say you close on the second of the month. At closing, you receive a proration of rents. If the month has 30 days, the seller gets 1/30th of the rents, and you get 29/30ths of the rent. Thus, the seller gets $93.33 of that month's rent, and you get $2,706.67. If you follow this, you'll know that you will receive a credit at closing of this $2,706.67. If the seller had each tenant put up one month's rent as a security deposit, you'll get another credit of $2,800. Granted, that part is not your money, but you still get this money at closing. Accordingly, you either take this $5,506.67 as a credit at closing, or you get a check for that amount from the closing agent.

But you still have to make your mortgage payment, right? No, you don't. Your first mortgage payment will be due on the first of the following month. What's more, your insurance premium (for one year) typically is paid up front at closing, and your property taxes will not be due until January or February of the following year. As such, except for lawn maintenance, you don't have to pay any expenses for the first month. Thus, you get a windfall of sorts—you receive a full month's rent (less the one day the seller gets), but you don't have to make any expense payments. Nice.

Almost any way you look at it, residential multifamily properties are the best, not to mention the safest, form of real estate investing.

FIGURE 2.2 *Comparison of Benefits of Different Types of Real Estate*

Benefits	Rental House	Flips	Foreclosure	Commercial (5+ units)	2–4 units
$0 to 10% down?	Yes	Maybe[1]	No	No	Yes
Affordable purchase price?	Yes	Yes	Yes	No	Yes
Right rent range?	No	n/a	n/a	n/a	Yes
Rent safety from vacancy?	No	No	No	Yes	Yes
Immediate cash flow?	No	No	No	Yes	Yes
Cash back at closing?	No	No	No	Yes	Yes
Economies of scale?	No	No	No	Yes	Yes
Fixed-rate mortgage?	Yes	Yes	Yes	No	Yes
30-year term?	Yes	Yes	Yes	No	Yes
Interest rate?	Normal	Normal	Normal	Worst	Best[2]
Homestead available?[3]	No	No	No	No	Yes

[1] While you could buy a house to flip with a conventional mortgage at 5 to 10 percent down, the competition will be offering an all-cash offer with a closing in a few days. Thus, to compete with these investors you would need to pay all cash up front.

[2] Because you can live in one of the units, you can get an "owner-occupied" mortgage rate, which is the lowest.

[3] If a property is an owner-occupied residential dwelling, the owner may file for a homestead exemption, which lowers the annual property taxes.

Figure 2.2 shows a recap of the pros and cons of each type of real estate investment.

3

THE MAKING OF MILLIONAIRES

We ended up paying less than $6 million for a job [Swifton Village] which had cost twice that much to build just two years earlier. We were also immediately able to get a mortgage for what we paid, plus about $100,000, which we put toward fixing the place up. In other words, we got the project without putting down any money of our own.

On July 20, 1974, we . . . secured options to purchase the two waterfront sites from the Penn Central . . . at a cost of $62 million. With no money down.

—Donald Trump, *The Art of the Deal*

What is it that makes many real estate investors millionaires? Is it expertise in real estate transactions? Is it picking great locations? What about good rehab skills? Good negotiating skills? Finding "diamonds in the rough"? While all these are useful to building real estate wealth, they are not the most important aspect. What is the single most important factor in building wealth? One word—*leverage.*

Donald Trump is who he is because of leverage (good marketing skills and knowledge of the business doesn't hurt, either). The first quote above was about Swifton Village, Trump's first deal, which he transacted with his father while he was in college. They made $6 million on that property. The second quote was about Trump's second property, Penn Central. Trump's first two deals were transacted without using any of his own money. Used properly, leverage is your greatest wealth-building tool. Used improperly, it will eat you alive.

If you read the first two chapters, you know how leverage works. The less you put down on a property, the greater your return on investment (ROI) or yield. If you are earning only 7 percent on your money, you're not going to become wealthy investing in real estate (or anything else, for that matter). Good real estate investors earn upwards of 15 percent cash-on-cash on their deals. If you factor in appreciation and tax benefits, they are earning upwards of 25 percent.

There are two ways of looking at real estate investing. One way is to look at your appreciation over the years. If you invest for the long haul, your property will be worth much more in the future than the price you pay today. If you look at Figure 1.4 again, you'll notice that the national average for house appreciation over the past 25 years (from 1980) is 261 percent. The National Association of Realtors (NAR) states that U.S. homes have appreciated 6.8 percent annually since 1968. In other words, you can pretty much expect time to give you an average appreciation of about 7 percent per year. We haven't factored in demand or forced appreciation. Inflation appreciation alone is working magic for your net worth.

Property Appreciation

Let's assume that you purchase a $200,000 triplex and you hold it for 20 years. Using an average appreciation rate of 7 percent per year, notice the equity (or wealth) that time has created for you in Figure 3.1.

FIGURE 3.1 *Value at 7 Percent Appreciation*

Purchase Price: $200,000

Number of Years	Value at 7% Appreciation
1	$214,000
2	$228,980
3	$245,009
4	$262,160
5	$280,511
6	$300,146
7	$321,156
8	$343,637
9	$363,691
10	$389,429
11	$416,689
12	$445,857
13	$477,067
14	$510,462
15	$546,194
16	$584,428
17	$625,338
18	$669,112
19	$715,950
20	$766,066

Return on Investment

A second way of looking at real estate investing is to look at your return on investment (ROI). Using the property in the preceding example, let's say you put 100 percent down, or paid $200,000 cash. Figure 3.2 illustrates your ROI, or yield, on your money.

FIGURE 3.2 *Return on Investment*

Purchase Price: $200,000
Percent Down: 100%
Down Payment: $200,000

Number of Years	Value at 7% Appreciation	Return on Investment (ROI)
1	$214,000	7%
2	$228,980	14.5%
3	$245,009	22.5%
4	$262,160	31.1%
5	$280,511	40.3%
6	$300,146	50.1%
7	$321,156	60.6%
8	$343,637	71.8%
9	$363,691	81.8%
10	$389,429	94.7%
11	$416,689	108.3%
12	$445,857	122.9%
13	$477,067	138.5%
14	$510,462	155.2%
15	$546,194	173.1%
16	$584,428	192.2%
17	$625,338	212.7%
18	$669,112	234.6%
19	$715,950	258.0%
20	$766,066	283.0%

The ROI is not bad in this example, but it's not going to make you rich, either. Let's look at the numbers briefly to see what significance a greater yield has. Do you remember the "Rule of 72?" This rule shows that, if you take the number 72 and divide it by your yield (your rate of return), it will give you the number of years it takes to double your money. For example, if your yield is 10 percent, your money will double every 7.2 years (72 ÷ 10 = 72).

If we can do better than that, take a look at the time to double your money at different rates of return:

Rate of Return	Years to Double Money
10	7.2
15	4.8
18	4.0
24	3.0
36	2.0

Why is the Rule of 72 important to your wealth building? Because you want to be doubling your money, your equity in properties, as quickly as possible. The impact of doubling your money, consistently over time, is mind-boggling.

You've probably heard of the illustration of compounding interest with the doubling penny. As the story goes, a young man is offered payment for 35 days of work in one of two ways. He can either have $100,000, or he can have a penny that doubles every day for 35 days. The doubling penny is a much better choice because, after 35 days, his aggregate sum has grown to $342,255,206! That is the power of continuing to double your money. Of course, this formula only works with real estate if you have two things: a good rate of return and time.

The easiest way to get a better rate of return on your money is to use leverage. Let's take the $200,000 property and look at the ROI with only 10 percent down. Figure 3.3 shows the dramatic result of using 10:1 leverage to increase the ROI.

These numbers are excellent, but some people don't have 20 years to play this out. You may need to set yourself up for retirement in only 10 or 15 years. To get there faster, you'll need to increase your yield even more. One way to do this is to put less money down and use more leverage. For example, if you put down just 5 percent, your ROI doubles. With 5 percent down, in

FIGURE 3.3   *Using 10:1 Leverage to Increase the ROI*

Purchase Price: $200,000
Percent Down: 10%
Down Payment: $20,000

Number of Years	Value at 7% Appreciation	Return on Investment (ROI)
1	$214,000	70%
2	$228,980	145%
3	$245,009	225%
4	$262,160	311%
5	$280,511	403%
6	$300,146	501%
7	$321,156	606%
8	$343,637	718%
9	$363,691	818%
10	$389,429	947%
11	$416,689	1083%
12	$445,857	1229%
13	$477,067	1385%
14	$510,462	1552%
15	$546,194	1731%
16	$584,428	1922%
17	$625,338	2127%
18	$669,112	2346%
19	$715,950	2580%
20	$766,066	2830%

year one your return would be a phenomenal 140 percent. The problem with that is the less you put down, the more risk you have. Depending on your purchase price and the rents in your area, once you get below 10 percent down, it's very difficult to cash-flow the property. As such, let's stay with 10 percent down and look at other ways to increase our ROI.

FIGURE 3.4 *Results of Increasing Demand and Forced Appreciation*

Purchase Price: $200,000
Percent Down: 10%
Down Payment: $20,000

Number of Years	Value at 12% Appreciation	Added Value with Rehab (20%)	Total Value	Total Gain	Total ROI
1	$224,000	$40,000	$264,000	$64,000	320%
2	$295,680	n/a	$295,680	$95,680	478.4%
3	$311,161	n/a	$311,161	$111,161	555.8%
4	$348,500	n/a	$348,500	$148,500	742.5%
5	$390,320	n/a	$390,500	$190,500	952.5%

Increasing ROI with Demand Appreciation and Forced Appreciation

So far we've looked only at inflation appreciation and leverage. What if we can increase our return with demand appreciation and forced appreciation? Let's continue to use the 7 percent inflation appreciation and the 10:1 leverage (10 percent down). But let's now add to the value of the property an additional 5 percent of demand appreciation (total appreciation of 12 percent) by picking a property in a hot area of town. And let's also add 20 percent in year one by rehabbing the property. Figure 3.4 illustrates the results.

In just five years we've turned our $20,000 into $210,500 ($190,500 plus our original $20,000). You likely have two questions at this point. First, you may notice that our biggest equity jump will be after our rehab in year one. We really can rehab only once, so we lose that appreciation fulcrum for this property after year one. Because of this, some may want to consider selling shortly after year one. A second reason to sell after year one, and not before, is because you will receive long-term capital gains treatment (15 percent tax rate) if you hold at least one year. If you are living in the property, you'll want to sell after year two (or later) so that you can capture the first $250,000 gain tax-free (or $500,000 for married couples).

A second question you may have is whether this kind of return and jump in equity is possible. While a number of factors will come into play (i.e., your city's appreciation, your down payment, the extent of your rehab, the rents for your area, the market GRM for your area, etc.), I can assure you that this scenario is very possible.

Let's start with the inflation appreciation figure. Since 1968 the *national* average is 6.8 percent per year. However, in 2005 (from June 30, 2004, to June 30, 2005) the national average was 13.43 percent (see Figure 1.4). Now that cuts both ways. If you live in Nevada, Arizona, Hawaii, California, Florida, the District of Columbia, Maryland, or Virginia, which all averaged more than 20 percent appreciation in 2005, the 13.43 percent figure is low. But if you live in Texas, Indiana, Ohio, or Michigan, whose 2005 appreciation ranged from 4.68 percent to 4.93 percent, respectively, even the national historic average of 6.8 percent is high. In those states you'll have to find demand appreciation and undertake some rehab to force appreciation. Actually, *everyone* should be looking for all three kinds of appreciation. Keep in mind also that things such as cash flow (which is better in the states with low appreciation) and tax savings have to be factored in.

Now let's talk about demand appreciation. Is an extra 5 percent realistic for a hot area? Remember my stories about properties in Thornton Park and New Smyrna Beach? They are appreciating right now at *25 percent* per year. That will cool, of course, but it raises the overall appreciation average of these areas to at least 16 percent over the past decade. Ten years ago in Orlando the hot areas were Winter Park and Orwin Manor. Ten years before that it was College Park. My point is that every city has areas of town that appreciate faster than others. When I lived in Atlanta, the hot area was Buckhead, and the up-and-coming area was Midtown. Like the hot areas of Orlando, these were the places where the yuppies wanted to live. If you live on the outskirts of your town, you may want to buy closer in so that you can get better appreciation in one of these areas.

Now what about forcing appreciation by rehabbing our properties? I've used 20 percent as my appreciation increase factor. Is that high? I don't think so. Not if you are buying residential multifamily units, rehabbing them cosmetically, and understand the concept of GRM as I've outlined it in this book. I bought my Thornton Park quad for $390,000, the top of the market at the time, and had it appraised for $520,000 a year later. If my $130,000 equity jump was entirely the result of rehab, I would have forced an appreciation of 33.5 percent.

Obviously, I can't know for sure exactly how it breaks down. If the rehab was only responsible for 20 percent of appreciation, that's $78,000 of my $130,000 in equity. Because I bought at the top of the market and the demand appreciation had not yet taken off, I presume that my forced appreciation was more than 20 percent. Perhaps the forced appreciation accounted for 22.5 percent of the value increase, and inflation and demand appreciation accounted for 11 percent. In short, the numbers used for the chart may be aggressive, but they are possible, at least over the short term.

You may think that averaging 12 percent appreciation, or a 20 percent return on investment, is unlikely, if not impossible. If you are in a low appreciation market and just sit on a property for 20 years, it probably is. However, if you are using leverage, forcing appreciation, and pyramiding up, it is very workable. If you get good inflation or demand appreciation to go with your efforts, it is expected.

How Leverage and Cumulative Appreciation Builds Wealth

I mentioned buying my Thornton Park quad for $390,000 and having it appraised at $520,000 one year later. Assume that I put down 10 percent, or $39,000 (I didn't). What is my rate of return for that year? Three hundred and thirty-three percent! What if I put down 5 percent, or $19,500? My rate of return jumps to 667 percent! One percent down gives me a return of 3,333 percent. I actually put *nothing* down so my rate of return is infinite. My point is that you can realize an excellent return by using a small down payment, making cosmetic fix-ups, and increasing the rents.

Now what about the second year? You can't fix up the property again. As a result, you can't increase rents dramatically, either. So your rate of return is expected to fall. This is one argument for selling your property after one year, or soon thereafter.

In fact, there are a number of ways for looking at your return after the first year. The most common way of looking at it, as the previous charts illustrate, is to take your aggregate gain and divide by your initial down payment. This is your "total return," not your average return. There are a number of flaws that make this calculation an inexact science. First, you have not factored in time (i.e., the time value of money). Second, you have not factored in later "investments" in the property, such as repairs or improvements. But trying to add in all these factors, plus time, makes this an arduous and inexact formula as well.

Another method for measuring ROI is to take your initial investment and also factor in your cash flow and depreciation, and the time that has elapsed. This method has flaws as well, such as missing the recapture of depreciation upon the sale of the property.

Still another way of looking at ROI is to ignore your initial down payment after year one. After that first year, your down payment is meaningless. For years two and beyond, your equity in the property is your "investment." That is, you could sell your property and use that equity to buy another investment. I like this analysis the best, although it's much more difficult to chart it through many years.

Let's use this third type of analysis and see how I'm doing with my Thornton Park quad. If I put down 10 percent, my year one ROI would have been 333 percent. The majority of the increase in value was from forced appreciation. Now we move to year two.

Now we have to figure out my ROI based not on what I put down two years ago but on what has happened with my equity from the end of year one. Notice that I had $130,000 in equity at the end of one year ($520,000 – $390,000). My new basis is now $520,000, with an "investment" of $130,000. I'm only 11 months into year two at this point so I have to use the current comps, listings, and market GRM to estimate the value now. If the property now is worth $750,000 (an estimate based on current listings), my gain in the last year is $230,000. With an "investment" of $130,000, that's an astonishing return of 177 percent ($230,000 ÷ $130,000). The return for year two is the result primarily of inflation and demand appreciation.

As an aside, let me point out the effect of combining leverage, inflation, demand appreciation, and forced appreciation simultaneously. In only 23 months, I've created somewhere in the neighborhood of $225,000 to $622,000 in equity, depending on how comps and listings are evaluated. Because I put nothing down on this investment, you could almost say that I created it "out of thin air" (more on that in Chapter 4).

WANT EVEN MORE LEVERAGE?

Technically, I may have created more than $500,000 in equity because I pulled out equity from this property and bought another property. Remember, after year one I refinanced and pulled out $48,000. With some of this money I purchased a second property for $392,000. In other words, I am leveraging my equity. Keep in mind that I don't pay any taxes on that $48,000 because it's not income. Because this money is loan money, I not only don't pay taxes on it, I get to write off the interest on it! Of course, I'm just transferring equity in one property to another.

And while time is going by, what is happening to the second property? It is appreciating as well. Based on recent sale comps, my second property has appreciated by $38,000. Because this property was purchased with equity from property #1, I would add this appreciation to my overall equity gain, as set forth below. I can continue to leverage the equity in property #1 indefinitely. In a short period of time, I'll also be able to leverage the equity in property #2. In December 2005, I bought property #3, a triplex, using some of the equity in property #1. This leveraging is how wealth is built.

This process is simple but effective:

1. Buy property #1.
2. Rehab it and increase the rents.
3. Wait one year.
4. Refinance and pull out equity to purchase property #2.
5. Rehab property #2 and increase the rents.
6. Wait one year.
7. Buy property #3 (and maybe #4) by
   - refinancing property #2 and pulling out equity, and/or
   - establishing a home equity line of credit to pull more equity out of property #1.

WHAT CAN YOU DO?

Can you do this? Yes, I'm convinced that you can. I'm not saying that you can get a 300 percent return or make more than $100,000 in appreciation/equity in year one. It can be done because I've done it. What I'm saying is that if you apply the strategies and techniques I've outlined in this book, you can realize returns of 18 percent or better on a consistent basis and build real wealth through careful planning and a responsible use of leverage.

Let's use a practical example. Say you have $20,000 to work with and you can get a consistent return of 18 percent. Using the Rule of 72, you know that your money will double every four years. Let's see how you come out over time:

Years	Value
Start	$20,000
4	$40,000
8	$80,000
12	$160,000
16	$320,000
20	$640,000
24	$1,280,000

Do you realize that $20,000 is a 10 percent down payment on a $200,000 house (or duplex or triplex)? What if you can buy a second one in a year or two? Granted, you're not likely to get an 18 percent yield every year on the same property over 24 years if you just buy and hold it. However, you may be able to get an even higher yield if you will refinance periodically or "pyramid up." I'll cover those concepts later. For now, just realize that your goal is to get the best rate of return possible, and to keep your money in play like that over the years. In addition, you'll want to buy properties every year (or two, depending on the size of your purchases).

Now for those of you in the low-appreciation states, you know the bad news. Your state averages just 5 percent or so inflation appreciation. But you know, too, that you can increase that through demand and forced appreciation as I've outlined. But the better news is that where appreciation is bad, cash flow is good. As such, your ROI will be pushed along by the positive cash flow that comes from being able to buy a property at a low price. There's always more than one way to skin a cat in real estate.

4

CREATING WEALTH
FROM THIN AIR

While Francis of Assisi was still alive, the religious order he founded, dedicated to poverty, had already started to acquire real estate.

—Robert Shea

The rich make their money differently than most people do. Most folks only understand money in terms of trading hours for dollars. You go to work, you work hard, you earn a paycheck, you save what you can, and you hope your pension or 401(k) program will provide for retirement. The rich, however, do not become wealthy by being thrifty or by regular 401(k) contributions. They become wealthy by knowledge of finance, real estate, and tax laws. In short, they "create" wealth.

For most people, this concept is a major paradigm shift. We've been programmed to believe that you become wealthy, or at least financially independent, by being frugal and saving. Don't get me wrong—these are noble traits. After all, in the bigger scheme of things, you don't really own anything; you are merely a steward of things for a while.

But it's a misconception that you can save your way to wealth. Do the math on your own income. Even if you saved 40 percent of your *after-tax* income every year, you still would not become wealthy. Notice that we must factor in taxes. If you earn most of your money by W-2 or 1099 income (i.e., job income), Uncle Sam will take about a third of that right off the top. If you earn your money from long-term capital gains, however, Uncle Sam will take only 15 percent.

People assume that high income earners are the wealthy. That's another misconception. None of the doctors or lawyers I know are wealthy. All the wealthy people I know are business and real estate owners. They came from normal backgrounds and average-paying jobs. They did not earn or save their way to wealth— they created it. They used their mind—employing techniques, leverage, and financial knowledge, and taking some risk.

Donald Trump transacted his first two real estate deals without any money down. He made $6 million on the sale of the first property (I think he still owns the second). Earlier, I explained how I established between $225,000 and $622,000 in equity in 23 months without any money down and without a partner. I did not "earn" this money, at least the way we normally think of occupational income. The axiom "It takes money to make money" is false. I didn't put down a penny when I bought my quad. I *created* this wealth by vision, knowledge of real estate, knowledge of finance, knowledge of my market area, leverage, and boldness. I did the same thing Trump did, just on a smaller scale.

Remember this: *"Wealth is not earned, it is created."* In fact, the more you watch rich people and how they make deals, the more you will see that wealth can be created, literally, "out of thin air." More often than not, the rich don't even put up their own money (or very little of it), as the Trump example illustrates. I never really knew that until I started representing several wealthy clients as an attorney and put together some of their deals. I noticed that they leveraged not only their money, but their time and their names as well. I also noticed that their backgrounds and professions could be very misleading. You would be surprised how many "good ole boys" who owned citrus groves, real estate, or a furniture store were very savvy when it came to finance and allocation of their money.

Wealth-creating techniques, at least in real estate, are all around you. But you have to see them with your mind, not with your eyes. I have shown you how I created wealth by acquisition of real estate. Here's another example of how I created wealth "from thin air" by knowing how to "wrap" a mortgage.

A number of years ago I purchased a home in Orlando for $297,500. I put down 10 percent so that when I sold it a few years later, my mortgage balance was about $264,000. The buyer agreed to buy it from me for $380,000, with $40,000 down, and I agreed to finance the $340,000 balance at 9 percent interest over 30 years, with a balloon in 7 years. This simply means that I took a mortgage and promissory note from my buyer, and he would pay me monthly payments instead of getting bank financing. If my buyer decided later to sell the property, he would have to pay off his mortgage to me, allowing me to pay off my bank mortgage. My underlying bank mortgage did not go away, of course. I simply "wrapped" it with this new mortgage. Here's what it looked like:

My existing mortgage balance (which I kept intact)	$264,000
Interest rate	7.25%
Purchase price for my buyer	$380,000
Seller (me) held mortgage	$340,000
Interest rate	9.00%

How did I create wealth, or income, from thin air? Because my mortgage note, the one I was paying on, carried an interest rate of 7.25. The buyer's note to me, however, carried an interest rate of 9. Are you beginning to see money coming into vision from the thin air? I wasn't just making money from the difference between my mortgage balance ($264,000) and the new mortgage

I now would be receiving payments on ($340,000). I was also receiving income off the $264,000 note that was not mine—I'm the payer on that note (the payee is the bank that loaned me the money to buy the house). You see, I'm making 1.75 percent on the $264,000 because I'm paying interest on that money at a rate of 7.25, but I'm receiving interest on that amount (because included in the $340,000 note) of 9 percent from my new buyer. This means that I'm making $4,620 per year on that interest spread ($264,000 × 0.0175). Did I work for that money? No. Did I sell a product or service for that money? No. It was created, well, from thin air.

While it may take years to develop a deep understanding of finance, real estate techniques, and tax laws, once you understand a new technique and use it once, you own it. You can now do it again and again. Keep reading real estate books. Join your local real estate club. Talk to seasoned real estate investors. Ask questions. Every new technique you learn will either put money in your pocket or save you money at tax time. Here are a number of techniques or tax law benefits that will help you.

TAX LAW BENEFITS

While I will go into more detail on the tax laws related to selling properties in Chapter 13, let me briefly mention all the tax laws that affect you as a real estate investor.

Long-Term Capital Gains

Let's say you own a property and you are thinking of selling it. Perhaps the market seems ripe to sell or someone has approached you about selling. You definitely should consider the market, but you also should consider the tax laws. If you have held the property for less than one year, your tax rate on the gain will be classified as "ordinary income." This means that your profit, or gain, will be taxed at whatever rate coincides with your income. For this example, let's assume that you are in a 33 percent tax bracket. If you made a $100,000 gain on the property, then, you'd be paying Uncle Sam $33,000.

On the other hand, if you held the property for over one year, you now qualify for "long-term capital gains." In 2003, the Jobs and Growth Tax Relief Reconciliation Act reduced the tax on long-term capital gains from 20 percent to 15 percent. As such, you now would pay only $15,000 in taxes.

Tax-Free Gain on the Sale of a Personal Residence

In the previous example, just knowing one tax law saves you $18,000. Is it worth it to buy a $20 real estate book every month to pick up one technique or law like this? Here's another: If you don't want to pay Uncle Sam a penny of that $100,000 gain, just live in that property as your personal residence for two years before you sell it. You now pocket all $100,000 tax-free. If you are single, you can pocket tax-free up to a $250,000 gain, while a married couple can pocket up to $500,000.

Depreciation

If you own a property, you know that things wear out. It's the Second Law of Thermodynamics—things tend to wear down over time. If you own a house long enough, eventually you will need to replace the roof, the carpet, the appliances, the siding, and so on. Because of this, the IRS allows you to depreciate the property. This means that you get a tax deduction each year for a period of time that the IRS considers appropriate to fully depreciate the building. For residential multifamily property, that time period is 27.5 years (31.5 years for commercial property). As such, this means that you can depreciate the building (not the land) 3.64 percent each year.

Let's say that you just purchased a property for $350,000. That purchase price includes both the value of the land, which is not depreciable, and the value of the building, which is depreciable. If you look at the valuation of your property from your county appraiser's (sometimes called the county tax assessor) Web site, this valuation will show what the county believes the land is worth, and what it believes the building is worth. As a general rule of thumb, use 15 percent of the fair market value as the land value.

Assume that the county lists the land value as $52,500 and the building value as $297,500. This means that you can deduct $10,818.18 each year on your tax return ($297,500 ÷ 27.5 = $10,818.18). This depreciation deduction will help to offset the rents taken from the property. However, you will have to "recapture" any deductions taken for depreciation when you declare a gain on the sale of the property. That is, any depreciation taken will be subtracted from your "basis," or what you paid for the property. Therefore, talk to your tax advisor about your long-term plans for the property upon purchase.

Keep in mind one other aspect of "creating wealth from thin air" with regard to depreciation. In most cases, you will be putting down 5 to 20 percent of the purchase price when you buy the property. However, you get to deduct 100 percent of the asset. In other words, even though you put down only 5 to 20 percent of the building's value, you get 100 percent of the depreciation deduction, just as if you had paid $350,000 cash for the building. It's just another combination of benefits—leverage and tax laws—working together to make you rich.

Management Deduction

Qualified individuals also may write off up to $25,000 per year against salaries or other nonpassive income. However, the property owner must meet the following qualifications:

1. The owner must own the property and take the deduction as an individual (not as an entity like a corporation, partnership, or trust). However, married couples and tenants in common meet this requirement.
2. The property must be a rental property.
3. The individual (or married couple) must own at least 10 percent of the property at all times.
4. The maximum deduction of $25,000 is phased out as the owner's income escalates. So long as the owner's adjusted gross income (AGI) does not exceed $100,000, he or she may deduct the full $25,000. However, as the owner's AGI exceeds $100,000, the owner loses $1 in deduction for every $2 that his or her income exceeds $100,000. The owner loses the write-off entirely once his or her AGI reaches $150,000.
5. The owner must be active in the management of the property. This activity could include screening and placing new tenants, collecting rents, and supervising repairs and maintenance. The owner could even employ a management company, so long as the owner continued to make the major decisions affecting the property.

1031 Exchange

A disadvantage of selling a property is that you are taxed on your gain, or profit. As mentioned earlier, if you live in the property for two years you can receive the first $250,000 of gain tax-free as an individual, or $500,000 as a married couple. But what if this property is not your residence? Not to fear, for the IRS offers real estate investors a tremendous wealth-building technique called a 1031 exchange (also known as a "like-kind exchange").

This tax rule allows you to sell your income property and delay taxation of the gain indefinitely. As long as you reinvest your sale proceeds in another income-producing property within 180 days from the date of sale, your tax liability is delayed. That is, your tax liability continues to "run" with your properties and you will eventually pay it when you sell your last property without reinvesting again. Your accountant will tell you that you are winning the tax game because you have delayed your tax payment for decades, while you've had the use of that money to create even more wealth. You can delay your gain indefinitely this way, pyramiding up, as they say, to larger and larger properties. There are a number of IRS qualifying rules for the 1031 exchange, such as using an independent agent to hold your sale proceeds while you search for your next property. See Chapter 13 for the technical rules of qualifying under this rule.

BUYING TECHNIQUES

Use a Buyer-Broker

Although I will discuss the pros and cons of using a broker in detail in Chapter 6, you may want to consider using a "buyer-broker" when purchasing your properties. There are two types of buyer-brokers. The first type of buyer-broker is the one who works for you on an hourly or flat-fee basis. You, the buyer, pay this broker. If you don't close on any property, you still owe this broker money. I do not recommend this type of broker. If you are reading this book, you are sufficiently knowledgeable to evaluate prospective real estate deals on your own. Almost all real estate investors possess far more experience evaluating and owning income property than do residential brokers or agents.

The second type of buyer-broker is one who splits (not necessarily 50/50, however) his or her commission with the buyer. Not every market has this type of broker, however. If you are unsure whether your market has this type, look at the broker ads in real estate publications such as *Homes & Land Magazine*. If you have this type of buyer-broker in your market, he or she usually will advertise here.

Here's how these brokers work. Residential real estate commissions normally run 5 to 7 percent of the sales price. The brokers for the buyer and seller typically split this commission. If the listing commission is 6 percent, then each broker is paid 3 percent of the purchase price from the seller's proceeds at closing. If you use a normal broker, you receive none of this commission. If you use a buyer-broker, however, you would get up to one-half of your broker's commission, or 1.5 percent of the purchase price. Let's look at the numbers.

When I purchased my quad in Thornton Park and my condo on New Smyrna Beach, I used the same buyer-broker. My purchase prices were $390,000 and $392,000, respectively. If I had used a normal broker, I would have received nothing from the listing commissions. However, because I did use a buyer-broker, I received 1.5 percent of these purchase prices, or $5,850 from the quad and $5,880 from the condo. I made $11,730 on just two closings. Normally, the commission rebate is either credited to the buyer's part of the closing statement (meaning that you put less money down) or you get a check from the broker the following week.

Some will argue that the service you receive from a buyer-broker will not be as good as with a normal broker. This is probably true. While I'll discuss the pros and cons of brokers in more detail in Chapter 6, just notice for now that you have a nice financial windfall if you do use a buyer-broker. I don't use buyer-brokers for market or evaluation advice; I use these brokers to receive that

1.5 percent commission rebate. I'm doing my own research and evaluation anyway, so why not get $11,730 "free money"? By using a buyer-broker, I created $11,730 from "thin air" as it were.

Close on the Second or Third of the Month

This is a subtle technique to create a little more money for you at the closing table. Almost all residential real estate leases require rent to be paid on the first of each month. At the closing table, rents are prorated. For example, assume that you are buying a quad with rents of $700 per unit, or $2,800 per month. Let's say that your closing date is March 21. This means that the seller gets to keep the rent allocated to the first 20 days in March, while you get the last 11 days. Your portion of that is $993.55 ($90.32/day).

But what if you closed on March 2 instead (allowing the seller to collect the rents on the first)? In that case, the seller would receive $90.32 and you would receive $2,709.68. By closing on the second instead of the 21st, you gave yourself an added bonus of $1,716.13. Here's why this is important—you won't have a mortgage payment that month. Your first mortgage payment will be due the following month. So you receive rents for almost an entire month without the offsetting expenses. By closing on the second of the month, you've created somewhere in the neighborhood of $2,700 (less insurance and taxes), again out of "thin air."

Deposits

You also will receive at the closing table a credit (or cash back) for the security deposits of the tenants. This is not your money, of course, and must be held and returned in accordance with the terms of the lease and state law. However, if your deposits are $2,800 (assuming one month's rent from the last example), that is $2,800 less that you now need to bring to the table to close, because you will receive a credit for that amount on your closing statement.

Prorated Taxes

Just like rents, property taxes are also prorated. The owner must pay that portion of taxes that accrues while he or she owns the property. Likewise, you are liable for the taxes due from the remaining portion of the year. But taxes are paid in arrears. That is, your taxes for the current year will be payable in January or February of the following year. What this means is that when you close, the taxes have not yet been paid. As such, the closing agent will prorate to your side of the ledger what the seller owes for his months of ownership during the year.

For example, if your taxes are $4,500 per year and the seller sold you the building on February 1, you would receive one month of taxes as a credit, or $375. This happens, of course, because a year from now you will be paying that money to the county for taxes which accrued during the month of January while the seller owned it. But what if you closed on October 1? You would now receive a credit at the closing table for $3,750, or ten months of taxes.

Seller Credits

There's one last way to get a little money at the closing table, if you need it. Often sellers will offer a credit at closing for repair or replacement of some items. For example, the building may need a new roof, boiler, or some other major repair cost. Let's say the cost of this item is $10,000. Why not just take $10,000 off the sales price? The reason sellers sometimes agree to having this figure appear as a credit at closing is to make it easier for the buyer to close. That is, the buyer now needs $10,000 less to bring to the closing table. If the credit is large enough, the buyer may even walk away from the closing table with money to put immediately into rehab.

These credits have been common in the past. However, lenders have become increasingly aware that the credit could be somewhat bogus, and could really just be an attempt to get the buyer to the closing table without having to put much money down (increasing the lender's risk). Nowadays, lenders often balk at repair credits over $250. What lenders typically allow now is a seller credit of up to 2 percent of the sales price for closing costs. As such, if the purchase price is $300,000, the seller may give the buyer a $6,000 credit toward closing costs. Rather than showing up as a credit on the closing statement, however, the lender typically will just move that item over to the seller's side of the ledger. For example, a $450 appraisal fee would be moved to the seller's side of the ledger as a cost to the buyer. The end result is the same—the buyer brings less cash to the closing table. If the seller ends up paying for most or all of the buyer's closing costs, and the buyer gets prorated rents and security deposits, the buyer may well walk from the closing table with cash back.

CREATING VALUE

The best way to create wealth is to create value. Value is created by making some type of improvement to the property. You might add a bathroom to a three-bedroom, one-bath house. You might change a zoning to allow for the "highest and best use" for the property. You might divide a parcel into two lots and sell them independently. Generally, however, the easiest and best way to create value in residential multifamily property is to cosmetically improve the property and raise the rents.

Cosmetic improvements are fast and inexpensive. They include painting the inside and outside of the building, cleaning up the place, landscaping the yard, trimming the trees, replacing old carpet, painting old kitchen cabinets, and replacing old appliances. Cosmetic improvements do not include putting on a new roof, replumbing or rewiring the building, adding a second bathroom or second story, or other major projects. If you are doing the work yourself, painting, cleaning, and landscaping may cost you only a few hundred dollars.

But don't let the cost fool you. A good cosmetic cleanup will give a building an incredible and beautiful face-lift. With a bright and clean new building, you can raise the rents for each unit from $50 to $300. I have raised rents as much as $250 per unit by nothing more than painting the inside of the unit (including nice glossy paint on baseboards, crown molding, and trim edges) and kitchen cabinets.

Remember that you are not just making it subjectively nicer. You are truly forcing appreciation on the property. The increase in value can be objectively measured by the gross rent multiple (GRM). The GRM, again, is one of the ways, perhaps the *best* way, that a residential multifamily unit is evaluated and appraised. When talking about 2–4 units, no one really uses cap rates and net operating income (NOI).

To figure the GRM of a property, divide the purchase price of the property by the property's gross annual rents. For example, assume you have a triplex that rents for $600 per unit and the purchase price is $250,000. The GRM would be 11.57 ($250,000 ÷ $21,600). Then assume that you cosmetically rehab the place. You now can get $700 per unit in rent, or an additional $3,600 per year. Your annual gross income has increased to $25,200. If the GRM is 11.57, then your new value is $291,564 ($25,200 × 11.57). By working a couple of weekends to clean up your building, you've added $41,564 in value to your building (and your net worth).

In addition, keep your eye on the market for the GRM in your area. If it goes up slightly, your net worth will go up dramatically. For example, after that first year of ownership where you improved the property, check the sales prices (and rents of those properties) of recent comps. You may notice that the GRM has increased. Let's say the GRM has increased to 13 for your market. Look again at your numbers. Your gross rents are now $25,200 per year. Multiply that by the new GRM rate of 13 and you have a new value of $327,600. With the stroke of a calculator, your net worth has increased again by $36,036. Adding this to your "sweat equity" for rehabbing the place ($41,564) would give you a net worth jump of $77,600.

So far we've only talked about raising the value through addition. You could also do so by subtraction (decreasing expenses). For example, many residential multifamily properties are on one utility meter and the landlord often pays the utilities. As you might expect, your tenants will be very comfortable when you are paying the air-conditioning bill. You may not think this is such a big deal but it really is. A few weeks ago I contracted to buy a triplex in New Smyrna Beach. It was a beautiful old house with a massive front porch and overlooked the intercoastal river. My broker inspected the property for me and neglected to look at the utility box (or ask about metering). After signing the contract, I asked him about it. He apologized for not thinking about that and checked with the seller's agent. As it turned out, it was single-metered and the landlord paid the utility bill. Because that monthly bill exceeded $400 per month, my break-even property now had major negative cash flow. I walked from the deal.

The quad that I live in was built as a large single-family home and also has such a single meter. However, I allocate the utility bill on a pro-rata (based on square feet) basis among all four tenants. Some landlords spend the money to have the units separately metered, but that is not an inexpensive project.

Keep an eye on things like utilities, yard maintenance, and property taxes. I'll just conclude with the truism that when you own the building, every dollar you save in expenses goes directly to the bottom line.

5

BUY AND HOLD, PYRAMID, OR REFINANCE?

It's tangible, it's solid, it's beautiful.
It's artistic, from my standpoint, and I just love real estate.

—Donald Trump

In the real estate game of residential multifamily investments, you have three basic options. First, you can buy a property and hold it for the long term, perhaps 20 years or more. This is the "buy and hold" strategy. Second, you can buy a property, fix it up, sell it, and buy a bigger property with the proceeds. This method is called "pyramiding." The third option is to buy a property, fix it up, and refinance it a year later, allowing you to pull out some equity to buy a second property while keeping the first property. All these strategies work. Every option has pros and cons, however, so let's analyze each in detail.

BUY AND HOLD

I know families who purchased large tracts of land in Orlando more than 40 years ago—the Duda family, with large agricultural tracts for their farm business in East Orlando; the Lee family, with large tracts of land underlying numerous hotels in South Orlando around the Orlando International Airport; and the Caruso family, with large tracts of land underlying numerous shopping centers and commercial areas just south of downtown. These families all purchased vacant land for what seems like only pennies on the dollar in today's prices. All these families are wealthy. The common theme for all of them is that the land or property was held for more than 40 years.

The best book on this "buy and hold" strategy is called *Buy and Hold: 7 Steps to a Real Estate Fortune,* by David Schumacher, PhD. Most people do not have the time to hold a property 30 or 40 years, but I highly recommend his book. Even if you are using one of the other real estate strategies, Dr. Schumacher, who appears to be in his 70s, provides much wisdom that is worthy of heeding. He built a considerable fortune by buying properties in the 1960s and holding them for more than 40 years. Let's review the advantages and disadvantages of this strategy.

Advantages

Continuous appreciation. Once you buy a property, the appreciation mechanism is set. It never stops. The same holds true for rents. When you sell a property you have a certain amount of time where your money is sitting idle while you shop for another deal. During that time you receive no appreciation, cash flow, or tax benefits such as depreciation.

No further transaction costs. If you sell your property, you'll incur transaction costs such as closing costs, real estate commissions, and title insurance fees. When you buy your replacement property, you'll incur closing costs again. You avoid this by holding your original property.

No capital gains taxes. Regardless of what you paid for your property, you won't have a gain upon which to pay taxes until you sell it.

Knowledge of the property. With a property that you've held for a couple of years, you know all the quirky things about it—the things that will need repair or replacement in a few years, and the service people who can take care of any problems. When you buy a new property, your information base is void and you may incur a few surprises along the way.

Mortgage payoff. Most residential mortgage terms are for 30 years. If you hold a property long enough, your tenants will buy your building for you and you will own it free and clear.

Disadvantages

Time required. With this strategy, you need to buy a property and hold it for a long, long time. Dr. Schumacher started acquiring properties when he was 18 years of age. If you own a number of properties at age 30 and you live until age 60, you should have a large safety net upon which to retire. The problem, of course, is that very few people own more than their own residence before they are 35.

Financially difficult. This strategy assumes that you have the ability to acquire properties at a young age. In most instances, it's harder for someone in their 20s or early 30s to buy properties because their wages are low and they likely have student and car loans to pay off. In Dr. Schumacher's case, he bought in good locations with little down and had negative monthly cash flow for *seven years!* I don't know about you, but I'm not too crazy about negative cash flow. If you happen to lose your job and you have negative cash flow on your property, you have a serious problem on your hands. Don't get me wrong—there are times when you may accept a negative cash flow to acquire a great property. I own a triplex that has a small negative monthly cash flow. I accept that for the same reason Dr. Schumacher did—long-term appreciation. You just have to be careful.

Lower ROI. As noted in Chapter 3, your ROI has its best jump in year one, when you rehab the property. You can force the appreciation of your property 15 to 25 percent by rehabbing it. However, you can only do this once. In years two and beyond, your rate of return on investment drops considerably.

Remember that in year two, your "investment" is no longer your down payment but your existing equity in the property. Because you can't rehab again to raise the rents, you have only demand and inflation appreciation to push you along. Your property still grows in value, just not as fast as when you can rehab and raise the rents.

Loss of leverage. Assume that you acquired a $200,000 property with $20,000 down and rehabbed it in year one. You've increased the rents and enjoyed good inflation and demand appreciation. You now have owned it for five years and you have $100,000 in equity. If you sit on this property you are not leveraging this $100,000 equity (unless you refinance, which I'll discuss later). However, if you sold this property (perhaps through a 1031 exchange to avoid a tax bite), you now could use this $100,000 to buy a $1,000,000 property, or two $500,000 properties. You again are using 10:1 leverage.

The implication of this loss of leverage is a loss of appreciation. If you sit on the first property, your appreciation is on a smaller asset. For example, assume a 10 percent appreciation rate. On a $200,000 property, that means gaining $20,000 per year. However, if you own a $1,000,000 property, you're gaining *$100,000* per year!

PYRAMIDING

The pyramiding strategy suggests that you continuously sell your properties and acquire bigger properties. For example, assume that you purchased a duplex for $150,000. Let's say you put down 10 percent, or $15,000, and the property has appreciated $20,000 from your rehab efforts, and another $15,000 from inflation and demand appreciation. As such, you have $50,000 in equity to work with (let's ignore transaction costs and taxes for purposes of the example).

Instead of sitting on your duplex, the pyramid strategy teaches that you "pyramid up." That is, you sell the duplex and use your $50,000 as a 10 percent down payment on a $500,000 property (or perhaps two buildings worth $250,000). By doing so, you have more than doubled your leverage.

Remember that your duplex was worth $200,000 when you sold it. Assume that inflation and demand appreciation are 10 percent. If you had held the duplex, you would be making $20,000 per year on your property. By trading up to a bigger property, you are making $50,000 per year ($500,000 property at 10 percent appreciation). Remember also that you already have rehabbed the duplex and cannot get that equity jump again. However, you can rehab your new building(s). This would allow you to force another $50,000 to $100,000 in appreciation. Let's look at the pros and cons again.

Advantages

Doubling leverage. By buying a larger property, your money is working harder for you. You are making more than double your money on the same initial investment (your down payment on the duplex). You have put your wealth-building program into place.

Opportunity to again force appreciation. While you cannot rehab the duplex again, you can, and will, rehab the new building(s).

Disadvantages

Dead time. After you sell the duplex, there likely will be some time when you have to find another property, or properties, negotiate the terms, and close. During this time your money sits idle. You have no appreciation, no cash flow, and no tax benefits.

Taxes. When you sell your duplex you have a potential tax liability. Unless you are using the personal residence technique or a 1031 exchange (see Chapter 13), you will be paying taxes on your gain. As such, I would recommend using one of those two tax strategies for each sale.

Transaction costs. As noted earlier, every time you sell or buy, you incur transaction costs (unless you get the other party to pay them).

Unknown property. Any time you buy a property, even with a good inspection, you may get a surprise or two.

REFI AND BUY

Is there a way to get the best of both worlds? Can I buy and hold and still pyramid up? Indeed, you can. You can keep your current property, refinance after a year or two, and buy another property with the proceeds. In fact, that's exactly what I did with my Thornton Park quad. During the first year of ownership I rehabbed it and raised the rents. Then, after one year (lenders require this time period), I refinanced the property, pulled out some cash, and bought another property of equal value (and later yet another).

In essence, this is the middle ground between the two other strategies. You get some of the benefits and some of the disadvantages of both. Let's take a look.

Advantages

Continuous appreciation, cash flow, and tax benefits. For the most part, you receive these same benefits as in the "buy and hold" strategy—continuous appreciation, cash flow, and tax benefits. However, your cash flow will be less because you just raised your mortgage payment.

No capital gains taxes. Because you didn't sell the property, you have no gain on which to pay taxes.

Tax-free, deductible money. This is a tremendous and unique advantage to the refi strategy. When I refinanced my quad and pulled out $48,000 in cash to buy another property, that $48,000 came as tax-free money. This is not earned income, it's a $48,000 loan. Thus, I don't pay taxes on it and I can use 100 percent of it. If I earned this $48,000 from my job, I'd have to pay income taxes on it and would net maybe $31,000. Not only that, but because it is loan money, I get to deduct the interest on it! I get the deduction, but my tenants are paying the interest (and principal).

You keep your money in play. Unlike with the "buy and hold" strategy, your money, which is your equity, is not sitting "dead" in your first property. You are putting that money back into play. Furthermore, you most likely have taken your money "off the table." For example, if you put $20,000 down on your first property, the day you refinance you have pulled your money "off the table," so to speak. That is, if you pull out $50,000 in equity, you are repaid your $20,000 and are now working with $30,000 of the "house's" (i.e., bank's) money.

Robert Kiyosaki, in *Who Took My Money?,* calls this technique the "velocity of money." Analogizing the refinance strategy to a poker game, Kiyosaki writes:

> A professional gambler wants to be playing the game with *house* money as soon as possible. While in Las Vegas, if I had put my money back in my pocket and only played with my winnings that would have been an example of playing with *house* money. The moment I began betting everything, I lost the game because I lost sight of my goal, which is to stay in the game but to play with other people's money . . . *not* my own money. As a professional gambler, I want to:
>
> 1. Invest my money into an asset.
> 2. Get my money back.
> 3. Keep control of the asset.
> 4. Move my money into a new asset.
> 5. Get my money back.
> 6. Repeat the process.
>
> This process is called the *velocity of money.*

Using tax-free, deductible money and keeping your money in play are two of the best wealth-creating techniques that you can use. If given the opportunity, employ them. This process is exactly what I have done.

Disadvantages

The "80 percent" rule. Unfortunately, you cannot pull out all your equity to buy that second property. In fact, you may get less cash back than you imagined. When you refinance, lenders typically work with an 80 percent loan-to-value (LTV) ratio. This means that they will lend only up to 80 percent of the new appraised value of the property.

For example, say you purchased a $200,000 property, fixed it up, raised the rents, and waited one year. You have the property appraised and you are excited to see that the new value is $260,000. "Terrific," you think, "now I can buy a $600,000 property with my $60,000 in equity." Not so fast. The new lender will give you only 80 percent of the new appraised value for your new loan.

In this example, then, your new loan would be $208,000 ($260,000 × 0.80). If you purchased your property with 10 percent down, or $20,000, your mortgage balance from the first loan is about $180,000. This would mean that when you close on the refi loan, you'll get only $28,000 back at closing ($208,000 – $180,000). I'll omit closing costs for simplifying the example. Now the maximum building you could buy would be a $280,000 building. And if you purchased your first property with no money down, you'll be pulling out only $8,000, which isn't worth your time or the transaction costs.

This problem, on the surface, is a major disadvantage of the refi strategy because you're losing the ability to put most of your equity to work. What's the practical result? Assume you sold the property, took your $60,000 of equity, and purchased a $600,000 property (or properties). If your appreciation rate is 10 percent, you're making $60,000 per year.

If you followed the refi strategy, however, and purchased a second building worth $280,000, you are making $28,000 from that building and $26,000 from the appreciation of your first building. Combined, they total $54,000 per year, or $6,000 less than if you sold and purchased a $600,000 building.

But there's more. You now have the opportunity to force appreciation in your new building. Assume that you can increase the value by 15 percent for each building. For your $280,000 building, that's another $42,000 to you. However, for the $600,000 building, that's an additional $90,000 to you. Let's summarize to illustrate the difference:

	Sell and Pyramid	Refi and Buy
Annual appreciation	$60,000	$54,000
Rehab gain	90,000	42,000
One-year gain	$150,000	$96,000

If we don't factor in taxes and "dead time" (when your money sits idle while you look for a second property), the "sell and pyramid" strategy beats the "refi and buy" strategy by $70,000.

How I Beat the System

Now here's where a good mortgage broker is worth his or her weight in gold. After owning and living in my quad for almost one year, I began looking at refinance options. Using the 80 percent rule, my refi option didn't look too enticing. Let's look at my actual numbers.

My purchase price, which was financed 100 percent, was $390,000. I received a new appraisal of $520,000 after one year.

Just assume for the moment that my mortgage balance was $390,000 a year later. Here's what I was considering:

Appraisal value	$520,000
	× 0.80
	$416,000
Less mortgage balance	− 390,000
Available for use	$26,000

With $130,000 in equity, that was not too appealing to me. How much property can I buy with $26,000? If I put down 10 percent, I only could buy a $260,000 property.

However, my mortgage broker used two lenders to give me access to most of my equity. Here's what we did. The first lender took the normal 80 percent LTV, paid off my original bank loan (and a small second mortgage the seller took back) with a loan to me of $416,000. That's 80 percent of $520,000. However, we had a second lender that was willing to take a second mortgage for up to 90 percent combined loan-to-value (CLTV) of the new appraised value. As such, I now could go up to $468,000 (90 percent of $520,000). At this point, I had access to $78,000 of my equity (less $5,000 in closing costs). Again,

Bank 1 gives a loan of $416,000 as a first mortgage.
Bank 2 gives a loan up to $52,000 as a second mortgage.

Bank 1 has an LTV of 80 percent.
Bank 2 has a CLTV of 90 percent ($468,000 in combined loans).

Bank 1 provides $21,000 in cash to me ($416,000 − 390,000 = $26,000 − $5,000 closing costs).
Bank 2 provides up to $52,000 in cash to me ($468,000 − 416,000 = $52,000).

To buy a second property for about the same original price ($390,000), I didn't need the full $73,000 available to me, so I took out $48,000 (although I didn't need all of that for the second property). Remember, this $48,000 is not taxed, and I deduct the interest on it because it's loan money.

Had I directly contacted a banker, he would have told me about the 80 percent rule and sent me on my way. Having a good mortgage broker on your team allows you to have someone working for you to find a way to get you what you need. If you can arrange the 90 percent CLTV on a refinance, it virtually eliminates the 80 percent rule as a disadvantage.

Less cash flow. When you refinance, you are increasing your mortgage balance, which increases your monthly payment if you are pulling out cash. In turn, this decreases your cash flow and could possibly turn your building from a positive monthly cash flow to a negative monthly cash flow.

WHICH STRATEGY IS BEST FOR YOU?

Like most things in life, there are some gray areas here. For example, you can buy and hold for a while and then refinance. When you refinance, you can pyramid up. But to distinguish between strategies, let's assume you are not blending opportunities for the moment. I personally do not like the "buy and hold 20 years" strategy (without refinancing to buy other properties) for the reasons I've outlined.

Tom Wheelwright, a certified public accountant who prepared a calculation for Kiyosaki's *Who Took My Money?*, compared the buy and hold strategy to the refi and buy strategy over a seven-year period. Wheelwright assumed a $200,000 purchase price, with 10 percent down, and a 5 percent appreciation rate. After seven years, your property, he concluded, would be worth

$281,000 and your equity would be $101,420 (including your down payment). Your ROI would be 58.2 percent.

Wheelwright then analyzed what would happen if you took some of your equity out every two years (he didn't state how much equity he was taking out, but let's assume it follows the normal "80 percent" rule) and invested it in another property with 10 percent down. After just seven years, Wheelwright estimated, your properties would be worth an aggregate of $2,022,218, with $273,198 in equity. Your ROI would have jumped to 180.9 percent.

I agree with Wheelwright's assessment that the refi and buy strategy beats the buy and hold strategy. Wheelwright did not compare, however, the refi and buy strategy with the sell and pyramid strategy. Personally, I like the refi and buy strategy the best, especially if you can use two lenders to refinance and pull out up to 90 percent of your equity.

Let's prepare a pro forma, however, for all three strategies, using these criteria:

Time frame	15 years
Initial purchase price	$200,000
Down payments ($20,000 on first property)	10%
Annual appreciation	7%
Forced appreciation	10% (first year only)

Figure 5.1 illustrates the result of the buy and hold strategy using 7 percent annual appreciation (the historic national average) and 10 percent forced appreciation in year one for rehab. For a savvy real estate investor, these numbers likely would be conservative.

Now let's look at the results of the refi and buy strategy (using only the 80 percent LTV refinance guidelines) in Figure 5.2. As you can see, this strategy is far better than the buy and hold plan.

FIGURE 5.1   *Buy and Hold Strategy at 7 Percent Appreciation and 10 Percent Rehab Added Value*

Number of Years	Value at 10% Appreciation	Added Value from Rehab	Equity
1	$214,000	$20,000	$54,000
2	$250,380		$70,380
3	$267,9070		$87,907
4	$286,660		$106,660
5	$306,726		$126,726
6	$328,197		$148,197
7	$351,171		$171,171
8	$375,753		$195,753
9	$402,056		$222,056
10	$430,200		$250,200
11	$460,314		$280,314
12	$492,536		$312,536
13	$527,014		$347,014
14	$563,905		$383,905
15	$603,378		$423,378

Finally, let's look at the sell and pyramid strategy. Under this scenario, I'll fix up the properties in year one and sell them at the end of year two. For each sale, I'll pyramid up to the point where the equity represents 10 percent of the down payment on the new property. In reality, I'll quickly come to the point where I cannot purchase a quad and have that represent only 10 percent of the purchase price. What most investors do is move up to commercial properties (such as a 16-unit apartment complex) and put down 20 percent of the purchase price. If I do this, of course, the yield comes down since I am using less leverage (a 5:1 ratio rather than 10:1).

The other option is to buy two or three quads. Because I am buying one at a time, and these are residential properties, I can continue to put down 10 percent. The greatest hurdle will be finding enough residential units quickly to use my ready cash. To keep the leverage at 10:1, after the first sale I contemplated buying

FIGURE 5.2 *Refi and Buy Strategy at 7 Percent Appreciation and 10 Percent Rehab Added Value*

Number of Years	Value at 7% Appreciation	Added 10% Value from Rehab	Total Equity
1	$214,000	$20,000	$54,000
2	$250,380		$70,380
Refi, pulling out $20K in equity, and buy $200K property			
3	$481,907	$20,000	$121,907
4	$537,040		$157,040
Refi, pulling out $69K, and buy $690K in properties			
5	$1,312,933	$69,000	$311,933
6	$1,478,668		$408,668
Refi, pulling out $200K (20% down), and buy $1 million in properties			
7	$2,652,175	$100,000	$682,175
8	$2,944,827		$874,827
Refi, pulling out $570K, and buy $2.85 million in properties			
9	$6,200,465	$285,000	$1,565,465
10	$6,939,447		$2,019,447
Refi, pulling out $1.49 million, and buy $7.45 million in properties			
11	$15,396,708	$745,000	$3,771,708
12	$17,271,627		$4,901,627
Refi, pulling out $3.7 million, and buy $18.5 million in properties			
13	$38,275,641	$1,850,000	$9,255,641
14	$42,934,436		$12,064,436
Refi, pulling out $9.5 million, and buy $47.5 million in properties			
15	$96,764,846	$4,750,000	$23,144,846

$950,000 worth of residential properties, which could mean buying two or three quads. When I get past year four, it will be very difficult to quickly find enough quads in which to place my money, so I've inserted commercial purchases and 20 percent down payments (i.e., buying apartment complexes) from that point on. Figure 5.3 illustrates this strategy.

FIGURE 5.3   *Sell and Pyramid Strategy at 7 Percent Appreciation and 10 Perecent Rehab Added Value*

Number of Years	Value at 7% Appreciation	Added Value 10% from Rehab	Total Equity
1	$214,000	$20,000	$54,000
2	$250,380		$70,380
Sell property #1. Buy $703,800 in properties (10% down)			
3	$753,066	$70,380	$190,026
4	$881,087		$247,667
Sell properties #2. Buy $1.24 million in properties (20% down)			
5	$1,326,800	$124,000	$458,467
6	$1,552,356		$560,023
Sell properties #3. Buy $2.8 million in properties (20% down)			
7	$2,996,000	$280,000	$1,036,023
8	$3,505,320		$1,265,343
Sell properties #4. Buy $6.3 million in properties (20% down)			
9	$6,741,000	$630,000	$2,336,343
10	$7,886,970		$2,852,313
Sell properties #5. Buy $14.26 million in properties (20% down)			
11	$15,258,200	$1,426,000	$5,276,513
12	$17,852,094		$6,444,407
Sell properties #6. Buy $32.2 million in properties (20% down)			
13	$34,454,000	$3,220,000	$11,918,407
14	$40,311,180		$14,555,587
Sell properties #7. Buy $72.77 million in properties (20% down)			
15	$77,827,390	$7,277,794	$26,927,835

As you can see, the refi and buy and the sell and pyramid strategies are comparable in results. On the surface, the sell and pyramid strategy appears to be slightly better (at least comparing the 80 percent LTV refi). Keep in mind, however, that this chart assumes you are buying a new property on the day you sold the previous property, which is not practicable. In reality, it may take up to six months to find a replacement property.

Remember also that the previous charts are not meant to illustrate exactly what will happen if you buy a $200,000 property and start on this process. Far too many variables are involved for any pro forma to be precise. For example, your appreciation rate may be 10 percent instead of 7 percent. Your rehab may improve the property by 20 percent instead of 10 percent. In the most recent example, I doubt that you will be able to find and close on $950,000 in 2–4 units the day after you sell your first property. In fact, it would be very difficult to follow the schedules in Figures 5.2 and 5.3 precisely. Also not factored in is your cash flow, your reduction of principal, and your depreciation benefits. Rather, these illustrations show you the dramatic long-term results that you can achieve investing in residential multifamily properties, especially if you refi and buy or sell and pyramid.

BUYING

6

USING BROKERS TO YOUR FINANCIAL ADVANTAGE

Gambling promises the poor what property performs for the rich.

—George Bernard Shaw, *Man and Superman*

Most sellers of multifamily properties use a real estate broker to sell their properties. In most states a broker holds a real estate license with the state. That broker may employ dozens of "agents" or "salespersons" to assist in sales. The agent or salesperson has passed a simple real estate test but does not hold a state broker's license. Instead, he or she holds an agent's or salesperson's license. Typically, the agent must "hang" (like a commercial sign on a doorpost) his or her agent license with a broker for one year or more before taking the broker's test and applying for a broker's license. In other words, an agent or salesperson cannot buy and sell properties without being under the umbrella of a fully licensed broker.

The main advantage of using a broker is to get your property listed on the multiple listing service (MLS). This service allows brokers from all over the country to see that listing and gives your property tremendous exposure. Some people also like to use a broker for buying or selling real estate because the broker may be more familiar with the market area and may be more experienced with real estate transactions than the buyer or seller. In many instances, however, this is not the case.

The experience and knowledge of brokers varies greatly. There is also a major gap in real estate experience and knowledge between brokers and agents. The majority of people who sell homes are agents or salespersons working under a broker. Most agents sell real estate part-time. They supplement their household income by showing and selling properties on the side. Because of this, most agents make very little money. In fact, they don't make enough to buy their own properties.

Because 2–4 unit multifamily properties fall under the category of *residential* properties, you most likely will come across agents that are normally showing, and familiar with, single-family homes. These agents typically are unfamiliar with the nuances and evaluation techniques for multifamily properties. Most of them will not be able to tell you what GRM or cap rates mean.

Real estate *brokers,* on the other hand, are more knowledgeable and more experienced. Even still, many will be unfamiliar with GRM and cap rates. If you happen to stumble across a broker who also *invests* in real estate, especially one who invests in 2–4 unit dwellings, you have found a very valuable resource.

In my area, I know of only three brokers or agents who have invested in multifamily units for years. I have worked with one of these three. His name is Jim Lyon. Jim is my broker for the downtown Orlando area (his niche). In short, he's the best broker in town. More important, he has owned upwards of 48 rental units and currently owns about 32 units. He became a millionaire by buying, owning, and selling multifamily properties and can give very valuable counsel on the viability of prospective properties.

Commercial brokers possess this kind of knowledge as well, but they don't work with multifamily properties under five units. If you run across a commercial broker with a Certified Commercial Investment Member (CCIM) or Society of Industrial and Office Realtors (SIOR) designation, take him or her to lunch. These are very sharp, extremely qualified real estate experts. They will be experts in real estate finance and knowledgeable about your local market (at least for commercial properties). While they likely will not be working with you to buy or sell your residential properties, they may be able to refer you to sellers and qualified residential brokers.

If you need a little help getting started in *purchasing* properties, find a broker or agent who invests in, or has invested in, multifamily properties. If possible, ask this person to show you the properties that he or she owns. You'll feel better knowing that he or she really does know how to help you. If you feel like you've got a handle on investing in multiunits, know how to find and evaluate these properties, or need extra money, you may want to consider using a "buyer-broker," as I mentioned briefly in Chapter 4.

Again, a buyer-broker only represents buyers. There are two types of these brokers—one who is paid an hourly fee and one who splits his or her commission with you. I do not recommend the former. If you don't close on a property, you still owe that type of buyer-broker money. Yes, this broker (or agent) doesn't have an incentive to "sell" you on a property so he or she can get paid a commission. However, this type of broker continues to get paid if he or she keeps showing you properties. So, the normal broker has an incentive to "sell" you on a property, but the hourly buyer-broker has an incentive to scare you away from properties. Both types of brokers have some conflict of interest.

The other type of buyer-broker is one who splits (usually from 20 to 50 percent to the buyer) his or her commission with you. Residential commissions are typically 5 to 7 percent. If the market commission in your area, for example, is 6 percent, the broker for each party gets 3 percent. Your buyer-broker gives you one-half of his or her commission, or 1.5 percent. On a $400,000 property, that's $6,000.

Think about that for a minute. Two brokers perform essentially the same service—finding and showing you properties. One broker gives you nothing at the end of the deal, and the other gives you $6,000. You could use this $6,000 to cover all your closing costs or to rehab your property. If you can find and evaluate properties on your own, you may want to consider using a buyer-broker to capture this "free money." However, one word of caution.

Oftentimes the buyer gets less professional service when using a buyer-broker. Here's why. Buyer-brokers have a business that is run, in part, on marketing and delegation. For example, a buyer-broker advertising that he or she will give one-half of the commission back to the buyer will have no shortage of clients. As a result, the broker cannot handle all of the clients. Thus, the broker gives these clients or leads to his or her agents. Remember that an agent typically has far less experience and knowledge than a full broker. On top of that, an agent working for a buyer-broker will usually get less of a commission because the commission is cut in half before the broker even gets his or her cut. The main reason why an agent would consider this is because that buyer-broker can give the agent many clients that he or she cannot get otherwise (perhaps because the agent is new to the business or less knowledgeable or professional). So do you get less expertise, knowledge, and professionalism with a buyer-broker agent? Probably, but it's not that much different from agents in a normal broker's office. There will be a huge difference, however, if you compare a buyer-broker agent with a full broker.

I don't use a buyer-broker or agent to get market or evaluation advice; I do that on my own. I use these types of agents to get that 50 percent commission rebate (in my area). So your options are as follows: If you need or want some help on finding or evaluating properties, use a broker who invests in multifamily units. If you feel comfortable finding your deals, conducting all your own evaluations, and you want or need that extra cash, consider using a buyer-broker. Over the years, I have used broker agents, full brokers, and buyer-broker agents. Unless you need the extra commission cash, I recommend using a full broker who invests in multifamily properties.

How Do I Find a Broker?

The best way to find a broker is by referral. Absent that, here's what I've done. If you are looking in a certain area, find a broker whose office is in that area. Independent brokers who hang out their own shingles have shown that they can survive in the business full-time and support an office. They typically try to work and develop an expertise in one area. I use an independent broker, Jim Lyon, because he has owned 49 multifamily units, and because he knows downtown Orlando better than anyone else. I think I originally found Jim from a postcard he mailed out about a downtown property.

The buyer-broker whom I have used I found through an ad in *Homes & Land Magazine.* However, since he does not actually take any clients personally, I've worked with three of his agents. I've bought well over a million dollars in real estate with this one broker.

I have also enjoyed the service of two RE/MAX Realtors. I used a RE/MAX agent to sell a property in Orlando and a RE/MAX broker to sell a property in Memphis. Both were exceedingly professional, diligent, and responsive. Notice that I used these agents to *sell* properties. Buyer-brokers don't sell properties, so there's no financial advantage to using one type of broker over another.

Why pick RE/MAX over other brokers? RE/MAX is a bit unusual in the real estate brokerage business. Most brokerage companies give an agent 40 percent or 50 percent of the commission that he or she brings in when closing a deal. RE/MAX operates quite differently. Instead of giving the agent 40 percent or 50 percent of the commission that comes in the door, RE/MAX gives the agent 90 percent of the commission.

So how does the RE/MAX broker survive? Each RE/MAX office *leases* space to each agent. For example, an agent might pay $700 per month to have an office and listing with a RE/MAX broker. The broker can cover his or her overhead by having five or six agents paying this kind of "rent." A good agent knows that if he or she gets 90 percent of the commission coming in the door, this will more than offset the "rent" fee. A part-time or unsuccessful agent would not want to work for a RE/MAX broker because he or she may not be able to cover the rent. However, brokers who have a "book of business" want to work at a place where they can keep 90 percent of what they bring in. The rent fee is just a cost of doing business, and is less than if they opened their own offices. Because of this, RE/MAX agents often are better than the "normal" agent.

Having said that, I have a great respect for two other national firms—Coldwell Banker and Keller Williams. While I have not yet had the opportunity to use either firm, these two firms have excellent reputations. Coldwell Banker recently expanded into commercial brokerage as well, and is now competing against giants such as CB Richard Ellis and Cushman & Wakefield (two of the best firms in the commercial brokerage business).

7

FINDING YOUR PROPERTY

For the right property, you can afford to pay top dollar.

—Dr. David Schumacher

Once you are ready for the hunt, where do you start? If you are looking for residential multifamily properties (2–4 units), you should be looking in the following five places:

1. Multiple listing service (MLS)—broker-listed properties
2. Driving around your area
3. Local newspaper
4. Commercial Web sites
5. Property magazines (residential and commercial)

I've listed these sources in my order of preference, based on where most of your purchases will come from. Let's look at each in detail.

Multiple listing service (MLS). The MLS is by far your best source for locating properties. The MLS is a national network for listing properties for sale. Every seller that utilizes a broker will have his or her property listed on the MLS. While most people do not know this, you can actually search the MLS listings yourself, without a broker. Here's how I look for properties now.

Go online to *http://www.realtor.com,* the official Web site of the National Association of Realtors. At the top of the page you will see a search engine called "Find a Home." Do *not* use this general search, since it will pull up only single-family homes. Instead, look to the right of the red "GO" button and you will see a link for "More Search Options." Click on this link. After selecting your city, state, and price range, you will see a section called "Property Types." Notice that all the sections are checked. Uncheck all of them except "Multifamily Home."

Now you can search and it will pull up only multifamily properties. When you run this search, you'll notice that the information is not complete. While you will find a photo of the property, you usually will not find the property address. Sometimes the rents will be listed and other times they will not be shown. Rarely will the annual taxes be shown. The reason for the missing information, of course, is because the listing broker wants you to contact him or her for more information. If you contact the listing broker directly, this broker doesn't have to split his or her commission. Don't do it that way. Just copy down the MLS number and tell your broker to check it out. Your broker can pull the actual MLS listing, which shows the address, rents, taxes, and other useful information. You also may want to search for other Web sites that give MLS listings because some of them will list the addresses as well.

For example, the Florida Association of Realtors provides an online search engine that will pull up any kind of listed property in Florida. In fact, you can search even by zip code. I have found the zip code search extremely useful because, in large cities such as Orlando, Tampa, Fort Lauderdale, Miami, or Jacksonville, you will find scores of areas that are great, but many that you wouldn't want to visit at night. For example, I can pinpoint exact locations that I believe are "hot," and all the competitive listings appear in the same grouping. In addition, because of the inconsistency of these

Web sites (sometimes you see rents, sometimes you don't; sometimes the listings are current, sometimes they are not), check both your state Realtors' Web site as well as the national site.

Using the MLS through these Web sites is my preferred way to look for properties. I can search any area with specific criteria. Often I can get the rents and the address. If I get the address, I can get the taxes from the property appraiser's Web site, and the exact location from *http://www.mapquest.com*. In other words, by the time I call my broker, I've seen a photo of the property, know whether or not the numbers will work, and where it is located. Thus, I'm doing 90 percent of the "finding" part within a few minutes each time I look. In fact, just minutes before writing this paragraph I found two triplexes and two quads very close to my beach condo (a trip to my condo becomes a "checkup" on a close rental property) by doing exactly what I just described. A quick call to my broker with the MLS numbers and he is off and running. He will confirm the rents, the occupancy, and see when I can take a look at them. It's a good system.

Driving around your area. The MLS will not give you listings of properties that are "for sale by owner," or FSBO. You will see those only by driving the area, and sometimes find them in the newspaper. I make it a habit of keeping an eye out in my area, and often take different streets as I go places. I do the same thing when I go running. Not only will you see FSBOs, but you may run across a listed property that you had not seen. I did this a couple of days ago and saw two properties for sale that I had not seen before on my online searches. By memorizing the street addresses, I can give them to my broker to check out or just do my quick online search.

Another reason to consistently do this is to develop market knowledge of the going prices. In a hot market, prices and GRMs change quickly. In just a couple of months, what you thought was the going rate now may be outdated. That's why appraisers don't use comparable sales that are more than six months old.

Many people sell houses on their own, without a broker. I have done it before. In my opinion, you can sell on your own if you have a high traffic street. I once owned a great little property (now a duplex) on a very busy brick street in downtown Orlando. I initially listed it for sale with a broker but the market was very slow at the time and the interest rates were very high. The listing agreement expired without an offer. I took it off the market for a few months and then decided to try to sell it on my own. I knew the street had plenty of traffic and many people would see my sign. I did not put an ad in the paper. Soon after I put a "For Sale" sign in the yard I had a number of calls. I sold it quickly, and for more than my previous broker thought that it would command. I think the sudden interest was because many buyers assume that they can get a better price with FSBOs because the seller will not incur a broker's commission. Normally, this assumption is true.

If you own a high-visibility property that you want to sell, you may think about this option. Otherwise, I'd go with a broker and the exposure an MLS listing provides.

Local newspaper. Most people who sell a property on their own (without a broker) are doing so to save a broker's commission (5 to 7 percent for residential property). To advertise, these FSBO sellers typically put a sign in the yard, and occasionally put an ad in Sunday's newspaper. I say "occasionally" because classified ads in Sunday's newspaper have become very expensive (not compared to a broker's commission, of course). Newspapers usually give you a set of days, like Thursday through Sunday. So most sellers will run this set of ads maybe twice a month.

I once found, and bought, a nice property that I saw listed in the Sunday newspaper in Memphis. I happened to be lecturing there and looked at the listings in the real estate section to see what the properties were selling for. It was a nice home in a great area called Walnut Grove. You might compare it to Highland Park in Dallas, Buckhead in Atlanta, or Dommerich Estates in Orlando (Maitland, to be exact). Here's what the ad said:

> **Hidden Treasure!**
>
> This house sells by 5 PM today!
>
> $60,000 under appraisal. 4/2 2,400 s.f.
>
> $150,000. Call Steve, 555-1234.

I knew that the "This house sells by 5 PM today!" was just a marketing ploy. I was interested in the "$60,000 under appraisal" part. If true, this was a very motivated seller. Indeed, it turned out to be true because the house was vacant. Whenever a house is vacant, the owner most likely is paying two mortgages, two sets of utilities, two sets of property taxes, two sets of insurance, two yardmen, and so on. I offered full price and bought it.

Commercial Web sites. A number of commercial Web sites exist, but the best one is *http://www.loopnet.com*. This is the site the professionals use. The leaders in the industry, companies such as Cushman & Wakefield, Marcus & Milchap, CB Richard Ellis, and Colliers International, all use this site to advertise their listings. Unlike other Web sites, this site is not an ad or a vendor disguised as a search engine. It's a national online listing of commercial properties.

The reason I suggest also looking here is because residential multifamily properties fall into that gray area between residential and commercial. Yes, technically, all 2–4 unit properties are residential. However, some brokers don't know this and think they are commercial. Also, brokers who do know of this classification also know that someone shopping for a five- or six-unit building might also want to look at the quad he or she has listed. In fact, in many areas a nice quad will cost you more than a ten-unit building in a less populated or less desirable area. You will find a few triplexes and quads, or groups of duplexes (that can be bought independently) on this site.

Property magazines. You may want to make a regular habit of reviewing both residential and commercial property magazines. Because residential multifamily property is seen as "between" these two categories, you may find 2–4 unit properties in both types of magazines. In residential magazines, like *Homes & Land Magazine,* you often will see duplexes or houses with a guest cottage or "mother-in-law suite." I often see the back cover of one of these magazines with a permanent ad by a brokerage firm that has a box for "income-producing" properties. In commercial magazines, like commercial Web sites, you'll often find triplexes and quads.

The upside of these magazines is that they often will contain ads on properties that are not listed on the MLS or in the newspaper. The downside is that, because of printing and distribution requirements, the ad you are reviewing may have been placed months ago. Nevertheless, these magazines are a good source for finding prospective properties.

Can I Buy Out-of-State Properties?

I have mixed feelings about buying out-of-state properties. I have done it. I have purchased rental houses in Kansas and Tennessee, and vacant lots in Kansas and California. I knew when I bought them that, living in Florida, the distance would be somewhat of a burden. When your property is far away, you can't just swing by on Saturday to take a look at it. You also can't supervise renovations.

When I bought the Kansas property it was at a tax deed sale and I bought it for a song. However, it needed lots of work and I wasn't going to be around to supervise any work. What's more, I didn't have any contacts for contractors or even handymen. As such, I flipped it. With the Tennessee house, it was in good shape and didn't need major repairs or much rehab. I found a property manager who had it painted, rented it, and managed it. That worked out fairly well. What I lost was the ability to go in between tenants and check out the place, do interior painting on my own, and otherwise keep my finger on the pulse of the property and neighborhood.

There are certainly pros and cons of owning out-of-state properties. If you are going to purchase out-of-state property, make sure you have a qualified manager to take care of the property for you. I am currently looking very closely at a quad in North Carolina that was referred to me by my Orlando broker (who owns an 8 unit property there).

Seeing with Your Mind

The real estate investor on his way to wealth must see opportunities with his mind, not his eyes. You have to see what others do not see. You have to see the potential of a property, or even a neighborhood. Imagine what a property would be worth in 10 or 20 years.

I mentioned in Chapter 1 a big but dumpy property in a fringe area of downtown Orlando that I considered buying in 1989. It was a huge house on a busy commercial corner of an up-and-coming area of downtown. Here's what my eyes saw—a lime green, ugly house that needed a ton of work. It was on a busy corner and would therefore be very noisy. It was across the street from a 7-Eleven convenience store where transients loitered. I imagined winos sitting on the 7-Eleven corner singing into the night. I saw the sleazy bar and Laundromat just a few houses down. In short, I saw an expensive "project" in a bad neighborhood. I wanted no part of it. Someone else bought it. I don't think it has been for sale since.

Today, that property is the crown jewel of the hottest yuppie residential and commercial area in downtown Orlando. For a number of years an accounting firm had its offices in the building. As of this writing, it is beautifully restored to its 1920s charm and is used as a men's salon. I'm sure that it is worth at least $1.5 million. The asking price in 1989 was $70,000. It pains me every time I drive by it, even to this day. If I had looked at the property with my *mind*, instead of my eyes, I would have bought it back then for probably $65,000.

Timing

J. Paul Getty is famous for saying, "Buy when everyone is selling, and sell when everyone is buying." This simple advice is a bit more difficult to follow than to observe. For example, in 2004–2005, the nation experienced tremendous real estate appreciation, in part because of low interest rates. The Orlando market sizzled. Sales were at record highs. It certainly seems to be a seller's market.

Because we saw record highs in terms of sales prices, however, many homeowners sold their properties to capture these great prices while the market was hot. "Who knows how long interest rates will be low and prices high," goes the thinking. I saw more For Sale signs in yards in the area where I live than I can ever remember. So was it a seller's market or a buyer's market? For sure, a brokerage company can tell you that there are only 6,000 listings in all of the city, and that's about half the normal number. In the first quarter of 2006, however, the market cooled (both in Orlando and nationally) and might even be a buyer's market. But for any given market, or neighborhood, does this statistic bear relevance?

The other problem with trying to time the market is that you may wait years before you have a clear "buyer's market." In the meantime, you could have purchased, rehabbed, and sold several properties. You haven't lost any money by waiting but you have a massive "opportunity cost" (profit that you could have made over that period by taking action).

In *Buy and Hold,* Dr. David Schumacher makes a compelling case that if you intend to hold a property for a long time, it doesn't really matter what you pay for it. You could buy it at the top of a seller's market, or even overpay for a property, but 15 or 20 years later it will prove to be irrelevant. The reason you can pay full price or even overpay for a property is because you are buying the future benefits of the property. Dr. Schumacher explains:

> In the final analysis, you should pay the present worth of contemplated future benefits, in which case you could be prepared to pay more than the market value. If you are right in your analysis, it doesn't make any difference. In 1963, I bought a four-unit apartment building for $35,000. Suppose I had paid $100,000 for it. It still wouldn't have made any difference because it's worth $1.4 million today. The key is to be right in your analysis of a property's growth potential.

Dr. Schumacher's point is valid. If you find a property with a good location, one that has tremendous potential upside, and you hold it for 20 years, you will be very pleased with the investment. I agree generally with this thinking. However, I must add one observation and one caveat to this strategy.

First, most of us don't have 20 years to wait. Dr. Schumacher started investing at a very young age. If you are in your early 20s, this strategy is almost foolproof. However, if you are in your 40s or 50s, you can't wait for Father Time to bring you wealth in 20, 30, or 40 years.

Second, if Dr. Schumacher *had* paid $100,000 for the property, it *would* have mattered because he would have lost it. That is, his mortgage payment would have been so high compared to his rents he wouldn't have been able to meet the debt service and would have lost it in foreclosure. Dr. Schumacher wasn't being precise, I know, because he was illustrating a point. Just bear in mind that it's okay to overpay for a property so long as you can cover the negative cash flow for an extended period of time. Dr. Schumacher admits that he covered negative cash flow for *seven years* before breaking even each month.

The Formula

If you have 20 or more years to wait, the buy and hold method works very well. If you don't have that long, refinance your properties every few years to buy more. Ideally, here's what you are looking for:

- A quad or triplex (the numbers work best)
- In a good or potentially great location (i.e., downtown, "yuppie" area, beach area, lakefront, mountain, not too busy or congested, etc.)
- Fully occupied
- Could use some cosmetic rehab
- Reasonable taxes
- Buy it at 7.5 to 16 GRM
- Be able to put enough down so you don't have negative cash flow (ideally, you want to put down 10 percent or less and have positive cash flow or break even) or set aside a reserve for a year's worth of negative cash flow

If you follow this formula and cosmetically rehab the outside of the place, and the inside as the tenants move out, and then raise the rents, you will be on your way to building real wealth. In most cases, you should be able to refinance your property in a year or two, pull out some cash, and buy again. Your wealth-building foundation has been set.

8

VALUATION OF YOUR PROPERTY

*Don't ever buy a piece of real estate without knowing the subject property's growth potential.
Ask yourself what it will be worth in 20 years.*

—Dr. David Schumacher

Whether you are buying or selling, you must be able to accurately value your multifamily property. Different valuation methods are used for different properties, and by different people. For example, if you are purchasing a single-family home, you primarily will be looking at *comparable sales* in that area. If you are looking at a commercial property, you most likely will be looking at *cap rates*. Finally, if you are looking at residential multifamily properties, you will want to look primarily at the *gross rent multiplier* (GRM).

So far, we've been looking at it from your standpoint, but an appraiser hired by your lender will look at it a bit differently. An appraiser looking at your residential multifamily property will analyze the property based on three approaches, in this order of priority:

1. Income approach
2. Comparable sales approach
3. Replacement cost approach

The *income approach* is the lender's best method to use for appraising multifamily properties. This approach looks at what the subject property brings in for rental income and what other properties in that area bring in, relative to their sales price. In other words, this is the application of the GRM. If Property A sold a month ago with a GRM of 10.5, your property is likely to be very close to that number. Your appraiser will add up your monthly rents, multiply by 12 to get the annual gross rents, and multiply by 10.5. I'll discuss how to figure the GRM shortly.

As you probably have realized, this approach is not perfect. Property A may be on a busy street or have dumpy units, forcing the rents lower, which results in a lower GRM. The estimated value of your very nice property will be pulled down by that comparison.

The *comparable sales* approach looks at the sale price of similar properties in your neighborhood that have sold in the past six months. While this is the primary approach of appraisers for valuation of houses, this method is fraught with problems. For example, the only "comp" in the past six months in your "neighborhood" may be just two blocks away, but located on a very busy commercial street. No one wants to live on a busy, dangerous street. Or your property could be an oceanfront property and the next comp is two blocks away from the ocean.

Second, the only available comps may be on a property that is not really similar to yours. What if you have a four-bedroom, two-and-one-half-bath home, fully rehabbed, with a massive backyard, and the only comps are three-bedroom, two-bath homes with small yards? How do you compare these prices? More to the point, what if you own a quad, a rental property, and the only comps are single-family homes? Do these really compare?

Finally, what does the appraiser do when there haven't been any comps in your neighborhood in the past six months? The appraisal process and lender guidelines require him to find *three* comps for comparison analysis. To find three, the appraiser has to keep looking further away, in different neighborhoods. As you probably know, neighborhoods can change drastically just a few blocks away. Nevertheless, the rules say "three" so the appraiser must do this. As you can see, it's not an exact science.

How far off can the appraisals be? I mentioned earlier buying a house in Memphis for $150,000. The seller had three appraisals. One appraisal was from a year earlier for $187,000. The other two appraisals, for $200,000 and $215,000, were completed within the past three months. A lender wouldn't use the first appraisal because it would be too old at this point. So, according to the "expert" numbers, the house should be worth, and sell for, somewhere between $200,000 and $215,000. I bought it and immediately put it on the market for $185,000, and then $180,000, and it wouldn't sell. I ended up renting it out. Just remember that appraisals are really informed guesses. A house is worth what someone will pay for it. Period.

The *replacement cost,* or *cost approach,* looks at what it would cost to replace your building. That is, if your building burned to the ground and you now had a vacant lot, what would it cost to build the exact same building? This is the appraiser's last option and is the least desirable approach. This method also has many problems.

For example, what if construction costs have risen dramatically over the past few months because of a lumber or concrete shortage? How does this approach take into consideration the killer location of your property? It doesn't. That's why this is an unreliable method of evaluation.

Because this book is not about lending, but about investing, I'll focus on valuation strictly from the investor's standpoint. The following are the recognized ways for an *investor* to value a real estate property or a particular investment. I'm going to list them in my order of preference. Again, you must understand that your lender's appraiser will not be looking at it exactly the same way. For example, a lender could care less what the property might be worth in the future. It doesn't matter if it's a beachfront property.

Lenders follow underwriting guidelines and appraisal formulas. So don't be offended if an appraisal value comes in differently (typically lower) than what you had projected.

GROSS RENT MULTIPLIER (GRM)

The *gross rent multiplier* is the "income" approach that appraisers use. In my opinion, the GRM is the single best indicator of value for residential multifamily units. Comps are helpful but every property is different, and is in a different location. Cap rates are useful for commercial properties but not generally for residential income properties.

The GRM is a figure that measures the gross annual rents relative to the purchase price. It provides an income-to-price ratio that can be used to compare properties. This approach does not take into consideration annual operating and maintenance expenses. The assumption here is that, particularly for 2–4 units, the costs for taxes, insurance, and maintenance will be very similar. To calculate the GRM, take the purchase price and divide it by the gross scheduled annual rents. Thus,

$$GRM = \text{Purchase price} \div \text{Gross scheduled income}$$

So, if a property just sold for $300,000 with annual rents of $30,000, the GRM would be 10. In other words, the purchase price is ten times the annual rents. Unless you have worked with these numbers for multifamily properties, however, a GRM number is meaningless. What if I told you a GRM was eight; is that good? Well, it depends on the area, and what other properties are selling for. Here's a general range for GRMs, and my thoughts on what to expect:

20+	Hot property in a hot area in a seller's market. Even if you put down 20 percent, you'll have negative cash flow. Appreciation should be outstanding.
17–20	Great property in a great area in a seller's market. You'll be lucky to get positive cash flow with 15 to 20 percent down. Another appreciation play.
12–16	You may have potential here. This should be a good to great area. You may be able to break even with 10 to 20 percent down. Excellent appreciation.
8–11	This is a good range to shoot for if the area is okay, the property is in decent shape, and the tenants are not too bad. If you have all three, don't delay, it won't last long. You should have decent to good cash flow with 10 to 15 percent down. Decent cash flow, decent appreciation.
6–7	This will not be a good neighborhood. Cash flow will be excellent, but appreciation will be bad. You probably will *not* tell your cousin that you own this property.
Under 6	You will not want to be here at night. Cash flow will be great, if you can collect it. Don't count on much appreciation; there are not many buyers for these properties.

Keep in mind this is a general range. You may find a terrific property with a 9 GRM because you have a motivated seller or a great buyer's market. Also keep in mind that you have to look at what other properties are doing. You may feel like your property is out of line with a 17 GRM, knowing that it will be tough to cash-flow. However, if all the properties around you are at 18 and above, you probably have a good buy. If you can handle some negative cash flow or put a little more down, this property should appreciate very well.

Also remember that GRMs change with time, markets, and locations. I have a book on buying apartments where the author suggests: "As a general rule, stay away from properties with a GRM higher than 7.5 unless you can be convinced that you got a real good deal." Good luck. Unless you are looking to be a slumlord or you live in Okahumpka, you never may find a property with a GRM at 7.5 or lower. If you live in a city, you'll be lucky to find a GRM on a decent property under 12.

Just before writing this page, I found 25 listings for decent multifamily properties in Orlando. The *lowest* GRM was 16 (I now own this property). The range was from 16 to 33.3. In my submarket of Thornton Park, there were three properties, two with GRMs at 25 and one at 33.3. I also checked properties in New Smyrna Beach. Those GRMs ranged from 13.8 to 30. The lowest one, at 13.8, I had under contract. I walked from the deal when I found out that it was single-metered and the taxes were going to be three times the advertised number. In any event, just know the going GRM rate in *your* area.

The GRM, then, is a way to compare your property to the market. Let me show you three properties that I found recently, including the one I had under contract, and how I analyzed them. They are all in the same city, New Smyrna Beach. I found all of them at *http://www.realtor.com*. I can see photos of the properties, map locations, the total square feet, and the rents. That's all I need at this point.

Property #1:
    Triplex listed for $245,000
    Total monthly rents: $1,300
    Huge property (4,080 s.f.) with good rehab potential
    Location: Weak to bad

Property #2:
    Triplex listed for $379,900
    Total monthly rents: $2,300
    Big units (3,000 s.f. total), great porch
    Location: Great—one block from intracoastal river

Property #3:
    Quad listed for $525,000
    Total monthly rents: $2,200
    Average condition, good rehab potential
    Location: Outstanding—one block from beach

So which property is the best? Well, that depends on whether you are pursuing the cheapest property (#1), the best cash flow (property #2), or the best appreciation (property #3). But how do we compare apples to oranges? By using the GRM. Let's take a look.

Property #1:
    Price: $245,000
    Rents: $1,300 × 12 = $15,600/year

$$\frac{\$245,000}{\$15,600} = 15.7 \text{ GRM}$$

Property #2:
    Price: $379,900
    Rents: $2,300 × 12 = $27,600/year

$$\frac{\$379,900}{\$27,600} = 13.8 \text{ GRM}$$

Property #3:
  Price: $525,000
  Rents: $2,200 × 12 = $26,400/year

$$\frac{\$525,000}{\$26,400} = 19.9 \text{ GRM}$$

What's the best buy? Clearly, Property #2, with a 13.8 GRM, is the best of the three (this is the property that I had under contract). However, this property will have negative cash flow until the units are rehabbed and the rents are increased (the negative cash flow was even worse when I found out that the landlord paid the $400 monthly utilities and the taxes were three times the expected number). Another option is to finance with an interest-only loan. That option might yield a slight positive cash flow. In a year or two, you could refinance and move to a fixed, fully amortized loan.

Having said that, the best *location* is Property #3, which sits about 100 yards off the Atlantic Ocean. As a result, it has the highest price, the highest GRM, and will have the best appreciation. Because this is a quad (where the numbers work the best) that needs some cosmetic rehab and is in a killer location, I considered this property, notwithstanding the high price.

Remember, I know this market fairly well, having visited this area for more than 20 years, and now owning a condo a few hundred yards down the beach. If I purchased and rehabbed Property #3, together with the beach appreciation of 20 to 25 percent per year, I think this property might double in value in five years or less. However, with a GRM of almost 20, the negative cash flow would be substantial. With 10 percent down on a fully amortized loan, this property would bleed more than $1,000 per month. Because of this, I dropped interest in Property #3 (upon inspection, it also appeared to need a little more than a cosmetic fix-up).

Why the GRM Is So Important

Did you notice that Property #1, which was in a weak to bad area, did not have the lowest GRM? In fact, because this was a questionable location (the seller's broker admitted to some crime "down the street"), the GRM should have been considerably lower than Property #2, which was in a great area. For the area that it was in, Property #1 should have been priced at a GRM of seven to eight. Without an objective measuring tool, you'd never know if this property, or any property, was priced right.

One last comment about the GRM. You will want to watch it not only as a purchaser but also as a seller. Let's say you purchased a property two years ago for $250,200. At the time of purchase, it had gross rents of $27,800. Your GRM, then, was 9 ($250,200 ÷ $27,800). Assume that you now decide to sell your property. For our purposes here, we'll just keep rents at the same level.

You have checked the sales and GRMs of other properties in the area. To your delight, you've noticed that properties have been selling at GRMs of 11 to 14. What is your property now worth, and at what price should you list it? Your decision directly affects the dollars you will put in your pocket at closing so you better be accurate in your evaluation. Let's look at your analysis:

Gross Income		Gross Multiplier		Value of Property
$27,800	×	9	=	$250,200
$27,800	×	11	=	$305,800
$27,800	×	12.5	=	$347,500
$27,800	×	14	=	$389,200

As you can see, you need to pay very close attention to what the market is doing with the GRM in your area. In this example, your property could have increased in value by up to $139,000.

Notice also that a slight increase in your monthly rents will have a dramatic effect on the value of your property. Assume that you purchased a quad in the previous example and that your monthly rents averaged $579 per unit. These rents were a bit under market because the place was not kept up well and needed some cosmetic rehab. You painted the outside and put in some landscaping. As each tenant moved out, you painted the place, maybe put in new carpet, and so on. You now rent out each unit for $625, just $46 more after rehab. This gives you only $184 (4 × $46) more in monthly rents ($2,208 annually), but look what it does to the value of your property:

Gross Income		Gross Multiplier		Value of Property
$27,800	×	9	=	$250,200
$30,008 (new)	×	9	=	$270,072

Notice that just a $46 increase in per-unit rent increased your net worth by $19,872. What if you could raise the rents to $675, or by $96 per unit?

Gross Income		Gross Multiplier		Value of Property
$27,800	×	9	=	$250,200
$32,400 (new)	×	9	=	$291,600

Now you've increased your net worth by $41,400.

Suppose that you bought in a good, appreciating area and the GRM goes up to 12. What happens when you also force up rents with rehab? Let's assume your $675 per-unit rents.

Gross Income		Gross Multiplier		Value of Property
$27,800	×	9	=	$250,200
$32,400 (new)	×	12	=	$388,800

The increase in rents, coupled with the increase in GRM, has increased your net worth by $138,600. As you can see, it pays to know your market GRM and the effect that a small rent increase can have on the value of your property.

COMPARABLE SALES

Comparable sales, or "comps," as we noted earlier, are similar properties that have sold in that area in the past six months. While your broker can send you MLS listings that have sold, you also can get single-family comps quickly by going to *The Wall Street Journal's* online real estate journal at *http://www.realestatejournal.com.* On the home page, look to the left side for "Tool Kit." Below that heading, click on "Find Comparable Sales." Now just enter the property address and the search engine will pull up the latest three comps. What's more, the engine also will produce for you very nice graphs for trends in your market (produced by Fidelity National Financial). See Figure 8.1.

If you do not have a comp within the past six months, the best thing to do is to look at the listing prices for similar properties in your area at *http://www.realtor.com.* While these are not comps (because they have not sold), you can get a general feel of market prices.

The reason I don't use comps as my first screen is because two properties could have an identical sales price, but a huge spread in rents. One building could have long-term tenants where the rents are under market, and another building could have high rents because it is much nicer or in a better location. Because of the rent difference, one property could have positive cash flow and the other negative cash flow, even at the same sales price.

FIGURE 8.1   *Comparable Sales for 2012 E. Harvard St., Orlando, FL 32804*

Address	Sold Date	Sold Price	Beds	Baths	Living Area (sq. ft.)
31 E HARVARD ST. ORLANDO, 32804	6/16/2005	$354,900	3	2	1120
10 W HARVARD ST. ORLANDO, 32804	6/23/2005	$249,900	2	1	1247
312 DEPAUW AVE. ORLANDO, 32804	7/26/2005	$350,000	3	2	1632

Single Family Trend Charts for Orange County

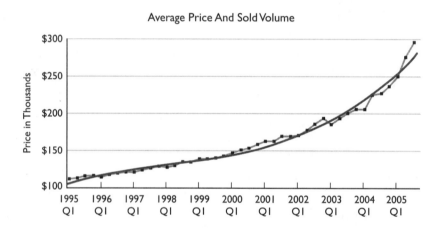

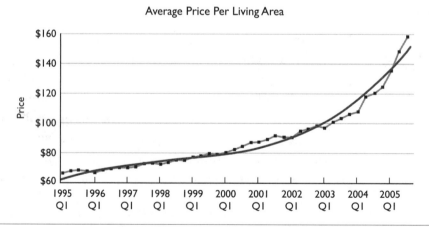

Source: Fidelity National Financial. Used with permission.

PRICE PER SQUARE FOOT

Another approach is to look at the price of the building per square foot. If you are evaluating a quad, for example, but there are no other income properties for sale in the area, you'll have to compare it with single-family homes. The problem is, the comps may be on properties with 1,500 less square feet than your subject property. In that case, compare price per square foot.

The other thing worth noting is that appraisers do look at price per square foot when comparing houses. Because 2–4 units are considered residential properties, appraisers will look at this factor when determining market value. After all, while there may not be another quad or triplex anywhere near your property, there may have been sales of other houses close by. An appraiser can't ignore the price per square foot on a house on your street that sold four weeks ago if there are no available multifamily comps.

CASH RETURN ON INVESTMENT (ROI)

The *cash return on investment* is your *cash-on-cash return*. This analysis measures the relationship between your down payment (and other cash you might have to put into the property, such as improvements) and the positive cash flow you receive for the year after all expenses and debt service. Other benefits, such as appreciation and depreciation, are not considered in this measurement.

Suppose, for example, that you put $25,000 down on a property (the purchase price is irrelevant) and made no capital improvements. After all expenses and debt service payments, your annual net cash is $3,000. Divide this cash number by your initial investment to see your cash return on investment. Thus,

$$\frac{\text{Net cash after expenses and debt service}}{\text{Initial investment}} = \text{Cash ROI}$$

In our example, then, we'd have a 12 percent cash ROI:

$$\frac{\$3,000}{\$25,000} = 12\%$$

With this simple equation, we can compare properties, even with different purchase prices and different down payments.

MARGIN

A *margin* analysis is a way of looking at a rental property to see your cushion, or safety, if there are any vacancies. This calculation is very helpful when you are comparing buildings of different sizes, for example, a particular triplex to a particular quad. Your margin is the difference between your net income when your building is 100 percent occupied and your break-even point. That is, this figure reveals how much cushion you have before you have to dip into your pocket to meet expenses and debt service. Thus,

$$\text{Margin} = 100 - \frac{\text{Operating expenses plus debt service}}{\text{Gross potential income}}$$

Your margin will reveal the allowable vacancy, or decrease in rental income, before you must make out-of-pocket payments. For instance, suppose you are looking at a property that has $31,000 in gross rents (if fully occupied the entire year) and $5,000 in annual expenses. Now suppose that your debt service is $20,000 per year. Your margin would be 19.4 percent. Let's review:

Gross potential income (100% occupancy)	$31,000
Less operating expenses	– 5,000
Net income	$26,000
Less debt service	– 20,000
Cash flow	$6,000
Debt service	$20,000
Operating expenses	+ 5,000
Total expenses	$25,000

Accordingly:

$$\frac{\text{Total expenses } \$25,000}{\text{Gross potential income } \$31,000} = 80.6\% \text{ break-even point}$$

Thus, your margin is 19.4 percent.

100% occupancy (100% rents) – 80.6% = 19.4% margin

The 19 percent margin, then, is your cushion, or allowable vacancy (rental decrease), before you have to make out-of-pocket payments. This margin, like loan-to-value (LTV) calculations, becomes very important to lenders, especially those giving second mortgages. You can use this analysis not only to determine your risk of negative cash flow but also to compare properties.

The higher the margin, the higher your cushion, or safety net. You might use the following guidelines:

Margin	Investment Potential
20+	Ideal
15	Acceptable
10	Too risky

CAP RATE

The *capitalization rate,* or *"cap rate,"* is the ratio of net operating income (NOI) to purchase price. To calculate the cap rate, divide the NOI (income after all expenses, but before debt service) by the purchase price. Thus,

$$\text{Cap rate} = \frac{\text{Net operating income (NOI)}}{\text{Purchase price}}$$

For example, a building with an NOI of $50,000 and a purchase price of $500,000 would have a cap rate of 10.

$$\text{Cap rate} = \frac{\text{NOI}}{\text{Price}} = \frac{\$50,000}{\$500,000} = 0.10 = 10\%$$

You can also work this calculation in reverse. If you are a seller and your NOI is $65,000 and the going cap rate for your market is 9, what is your property value?

$$\text{Value} = \frac{\text{NOI}}{\text{Cap rate}} = \frac{\$50,000}{0.09} = \$555,555$$

Historically, the average cap rate has been ten. If you are a seller, you'd like to get your cap rate below that. If you are a buyer, you want to get above that.

Keep in mind, however, that while this valuation method is *the* measurement for commercial properties, it is rarely, if ever, used for valuing residential properties. I include it here because you will hear of cap rates eventually. Once you move from four-unit properties to five-unit properties and above, you will move from a GRM calculation to a cap rate calculation.

SOME USEFUL AVERAGE ANNUAL EXPENSE NUMBERS

When you start running pro forma calculations to see if your prospective property will have cash flow, you'll need to make some educated estimates of expenses, namely, repairs and maintenance, property taxes, and insurance. While these figures will vary slightly, depending on your location and number of units, you can use the following annual expense estimates as your guide (until you get accurate figures from the tax collector's office and the seller):

Repairs and maintenance	9% of rents
Property taxes	$0.015 \times$ fair market value
Insurance	$0.005 \times$ fair market value

Once you have a handle on expenses and expected rents, you will know exactly what your cash flow will be. If the numbers still work after factoring in your debt service, you are ready to check out the property and make an offer.

9

VERIFICATION AND DUE DILIGENCE

Trust, but verify.

—President Ronald Reagan (on negotiating with the Soviet Union)

Once you've made a quick financial analysis using the GRM, if the property looks good, you'll want to prepare a full analysis of the property. If the seller was selling a 20-unit apartment complex, the seller's broker would prepare a very detailed breakdown of annual expenses and rents. This detailed information goes by several names:

1. Annual Property Operating Data (APOD) statement
2. Setup sheet
3. Investment property fact sheet
4. Income statement

ANNUAL PROPERTY OPERATING DATA

The listing broker, with the seller's assistance, will include in this statement all the annual income and expenses for the property. This statement should be very detailed, showing the actual figures for expenses such as taxes, maintenance, repairs, insurance, utilities, and advertising, while including an income adjustment (typically 5 percent) for vacancy. Figure 9.1 provides an example of an APOD. The more professional the broker you are dealing with, the more complete this form will be.

Oftentimes, brokers will give you a pro forma statement. *Pro forma* is Latin for "looking forward." Ignore it. If the numbers were good in the past year, the broker would be using those. But brokers want to shed the property in its best light, so very good pro forma numbers may be shown as if they actually occurred. What pro forma really means is this: "These are the best possible numbers you could get if you rehabbed the entire complex, charged maximum rent, had no vacancies, nothing broke, you mowed the lawn yourself, and you paid no management fees." In other words, ignore any pro forma estimates and get actual figures from the seller. The purchase price should not be set on what the property *might* do, but on what it historically *has* done.

Having said all this, know that you'll never see an APOD if you stay with 2–4 unit purchases. These statements are not given by sellers or brokers for residential properties. What you may get is an MLS listing report, showing rent per unit, and some general figures such as square feet, building age, taxes, and school district. For residential multifamily purchases, you must create your own APOD statement. I include this information here because you need to think at this level of detail, and because you will see APODs if you move to buying properties of five or more units (commercial).

VERIFICATION

The income is easy to determine: What are the rents and when do the leases expire? The norm for the industry is to show a 5 percent vacancy. For expenses, which must be verified during

FIGURE 9.1   *Annual Property Operating Data Statement*

ANNUAL PROPERTY OPERATING DATA

Property name _____   Owner/broker_____

Address _____   Phone no. _____

_____   Sales Price _____

Number of units _____   Year Built _____

Unit mix (bedrooms/baths) _____

Rent per unit _____

Current occupancy _____

Deposits held per unit _____

_____

INCOME   COMMENTS

Potential annual rents _____   _____

less vacancy (5%)   _____   _____

Gross annual rents   _____   _____

Other income   _____   _____

Gross annual income _____   _____

EXPENSES

Real estate taxes   _____   _____

Insurance   _____   _____

Maintenance   _____   _____

Repairs   _____   _____

Utilities   _____   _____

Management fees   _____   _____

Advertising   _____   _____

Other   _____   _____

Annual expenses   _____   _____

Net operating income _____   _____

Capitalization rate   _____   _____

Price per unit   _____   _____

Price per sq. foot   _____   _____

due diligence (between contract and close), you need to know the annual taxes, insurance, maintenance, and repair costs. In the past chapter I gave you some easy reference figures to plug in for expenses until you receive exact figures from the seller.

If you forget everything else in this chapter, please do three things:

1. Check to see what the current year's taxes are;
2. Calculate what the taxes will be at the current mill rate (you can get from the tax collector's or property assessor's office) and the sales price; and
3. Check to see if the units are individually metered.

I mentioned earlier a great triplex I had under contract in New Smyrna Beach, Florida. The GRM was 13.8, which was easily the lowest in the area. My broker inspected the property for me and told me that everything was okay. I made an offer and the seller agreed. We signed a contract. I asked my broker to double-check the current taxes and the meter issue. He had done neither on his own.

The seller's agent put on the MLS listing the taxes for 2004, which were very reasonable. However, what wasn't disclosed was the city's new tax rates that, coupled with the sales price, would have *tripled* the taxes. On top of that, my broker found out that, as I had feared, the property was on one utility meter and the landlord paid it—$400 a month. Surprise! Given these two surprise numbers, I walked from the deal.

Always confirm these two numbers as quickly as possible. Almost all brokers will list the prior year's taxes because the number is lower than the current year's taxes (which are not yet payable), and any pro forma calculations by a prospective buyer will come out better with the past year's taxes. If you are looking at an older house, built before 1950, for instance, just assume that it is on one utility meter. The question is, who pays the bill, the tenants or the landlord?

In short, you want to know if the rents from the property will cover all expenses and debt service. Hopefully, you'll have a nice buffer of cash flow. If not, you need to know exactly how much negative cash flow to expect.

Let's say you expect $300 per month negative cash flow. My suggestion is that you put $3,600 in a savings account designated to cover the negative cash flow for one year. If you are thinking you could add that $3,600 to your down payment to eliminate the negative cash flow, run the numbers. You'll see that reducing your loan principal by $3,600 will reduce your monthly mortgage payment very little.

Figure 9.2 contains my personal analysis checklist. This information is what I'm usually looking for to determine if I have a further interest:

DEBT SERVICE COVERAGE RATIO (DSCR)

There's one last ratio that you may want to calculate as you finish your analysis of the property—the *debt service coverage ratio*. This ratio is similar to margin, which we covered in the last chapter. This ratio will be particularly important to your lender as it measures your ability to pay the debt service. Here's the formula:

$$DSCR = \frac{\text{Net operating income (NOI)}}{\text{Debt service payment}}$$

Assume that your NOI is $50,000 and your debt service is $40,000 annually. Here's the breakdown:

$$\frac{\$48,000}{\$40,000} = 1.20 \text{ DSCR}$$

FIGURE 9.2 *Residential Multifamily Analysis Checklist*

---

1. Monthly rents: _____
   (Can the rents be increased after rehab?)

2. Occupancy: _____
   (I'm rarely interested if the property is not 100 percent occupied.)

3. GRM: _____
   (Is it in line with the market?)

4. Number of units: _____
   (Four is best, then three.)

5. Location: _____
   (Is the neighborhood going up or down? Close to a park or the "cool" places?)

6. Structural soundness: _____
   (Your professional inspection will give details, but does it look okay at first glance?)

7. Could it benefit from cosmetics? _____
   (I'm hoping it needs painting and landscaping.)

8. Does it have any "sizzle" features? _____
   (For example, wood floors, crown molding, fireplace, large porch, French doors, big yard, ten-foot ceilings, nice common foyer, antique stairs or woodwork, or great views)

9. Expiration of existing leases: _____
   (Any scary tenants or pets to deal with in the meantime?)

10. My expected mortgage payment: _____

11. Current annual taxes (and what they will be after the new price adjustment is made): _____

12. Expected insurance cost: _____

13. Expected annual maintenance costs: _____

14. Utility costs not covered by tenants: _____

15. Needed repairs or improvements, and cost: _____

16. Net monthly cash flow: _____
    (Allocate taxes, insurance, maintenance, and repairs pro rata for 12 months.)

17. Cash-on-cash return: _____

Your lender's DSCR requirement may vary slightly, depending on the lender's loan-to-value ratio, your strength as a borrower, and the type and quality of the property. In most cases, your lender will require a DSCR of 1.2 (but possibly up to 1.35). If your debt service is $40,000, as shown in the previous example, you will most likely need an NOI of at least $48,000.

$$\frac{\$50,000}{\$40,000} = 1.25 \text{ DSCR}$$

Keep in mind that when your lender does a calculation of NOI, it will use the lesser of the actual occupancy or 95 percent. It doesn't matter if your property stays at 100 percent occupancy; your lender will factor in a vacancy of 5 percent as a safety net for turnover.

If you look only at 2–4 units, you'll rarely hear your lender discuss this term. However, your lender's underwriting department may be using it. Therefore, it's good to know what they will be doing with the numbers. It's also a good analysis for you to do as a reminder of your vacancy risk.

DUE DILIGENCE

Once you have the property under contract, you'll need to move into your due diligence. Figure 9.3 sets forth my personal due diligence checklist.

THE INSPECTION

If everything looks good at this point, hire an experienced inspector for your inspection. Do not use your Uncle Fred, who is a good handyman or who has rehabbed houses before. Too much is

FIGURE 9.3   *Residential Multifamily Due Diligence Checklist*

1. Copy of rent roll: _____

2. Copy of leases: _____
   a. Matches rent roll?
   b. First lease to expire?
   c. Second lease to expire?
   d. Read all leases for unusual terms.
   e. Security deposits held: _____ .

3. Copy of county appraiser's information: _____
   a. Does the "use" match (zoned for current use)?
   b. Does the square footage match?
   c. Annual taxes confirmed.

   You should be able to obtain this information from the county's Web site.

4. Copy of utility bills: _____
   a. Are all units on one meter or separate meters? If they are all on one meter, as is the case with old converted houses, I divide the utilities on a pro-rata basis among the tenants.
   b. Any deposits?

5. Copy of existing termite bond: _____
   a. Does it also cover subterranean termites?
   b. Get a copy of this and review it. If this is an old wood structure, you'll be using it! Check what the annual renewal rate is.

6. Any existing inspection reports, survey, or appraisal? _____

7. Sales comparables: _____
   (Do this on your own.)

8. Interior and exterior photos. _____

9. Contact information for vendors: _____
   (Pest control, electrical, termite, yard maintenance, appliance, HVAC, etc.)

10. Any service contracts? _____
    (For example, termite, pest control, yard, home warranty, etc.)

11. Insurance policy: _____

12. List all personal property to be included: _____
    (For example, appliances, fixtures, furniture, etc.)

on the line. You need a professional. I just turned down pursuing a quad because the inspection report showed that the piers (part of the foundation that supports very old houses) were cracked and deteriorating.

The best way to find an inspector is through a referral. Your broker should have someone in mind. It's helpful to watch your inspector as he works. You will be amazed at the things he finds wrong with your property! Don't be too alarmed; every property has plenty of things wrong with it. You are looking for surprises or deal killers. The previous example with the structural problem is a deal killer. Termite infestation is a deal killer. Surprises are annoying things that you know you'll have to live with or spend a few extra bucks fixing.

A number of years ago I purchased a very nice home as my residence. It was in a very private, gated community of only 16 homes. The location was terrific. It was one mile from Isleworth. That's where Tiger Woods, Ken Griffey, Jr., Shaq, and Wesley Snipes used to live (Shaq still owns his house there, I suppose for his friends to use). It was a four-bedroom, three-and-one-half bath, with a three-car garage. It had 3,300 square feet under heat and air, but had a huge courtyard and pool area inside the house (not included in the square feet). In short, it was a killer place.

When I watched the inspector do his work, he was looking at the tub in the master bedroom. It was a massive Jacuzzi tub that overlooked the pool area. I generally prefer showers over baths, but looking at this thing, I couldn't wait to get in. Then my inspector said, "Oh, by the way, if you take a bath in here, don't fill it up all the way; the water heater isn't big enough to heat all of this water." What? The developer built this huge luxury house and scrimped on the water heater? Who takes a lukewarm bubble bath? What if someone just took a hot shower? Don't assume that just because it's a nice property with quality construction that there won't be some inspection issues.

Here's another example. I bought a quad that had a beautiful fireplace in one of the units. What could be wrong with a nice brick fireplace, right? My inspector had looked inside with a flashlight and determined that it did not have a damper. The damper is the valve midway up your chimney that controls the burn rate of your fire. Without one you have three problems. First, sparks could go up the chimney and land on the roof. That's a fire hazard. Second, when it's cold and you light up a cozy fire to warm the place, without a damper the heat will be pulled directly up the chimney and out the top so that you don't get any heat in the room. That's a romance hazard. Third, when it's hot and you have the air-conditioning on, the nice cool air in the room will be sucked up the chimney and pulled outside. That's a checkbook hazard.

These are the kind of surprises that only a professional inspector will find. Hire a good one.

10

MAKING OFFERS

One good tactic for speeding up a deal is to show a lack of interest in it.

—Donald Trump, *How to Get Rich*

Most people reading a real estate book don't need a chapter on how to make offers. If you are using a broker, the broker will be using a standard board of Realtors contract. In Florida, the Florida Bar and the Florida Board of Realtors together have produced a standard form that everyone in residential real estate uses. I provide a chapter here on making offers, not so much to give you new information but to dispel real estate seminar hype, myths, and errant information. It's quite amazing how many nonlawyers on the seminar circuit will dispense quite a bit of legal advice on real estate contracts.

Here is a recent example from a published real estate seminar speaker and self-proclaimed "guru":

> I am not an attorney or accountant, and I don't provide legal advice, but I'm willing to share the contract I use as a guide for creating your own. Be sure to have an attorney check it out for you. When you visit your attor-

ney, say: "I'm using this basic contract that came from [seminar "guru"] as a boilerplate. I want to include the important points from the state contract. Can you help me do this?" Have your attorney point out the important points and then type them into your contract.

This is the common advice of most real estate seminar gurus and is almost word for word what you will hear. The reason the pitch is the same is because it's a pitch. In essence, here's the guru's marketing hook:

You need to buy my software/contracts because the standard form will not protect you. It will not protect you because
1. it is set up as a "neutral" document, "even" for both sides; and
2. your attorney is not as savvy a real estate expert as I am.

This reasoning helps to overcome the waiting objection, "I have a contract from my broker (or attorney), so why do I need this one?" The problem the guru has, of course, is that every state has certain clauses that are inserted either because they are required by state law or from years of case law (i.e., litigation over a specified point). The guru has to find a way to get you to buy his form/software and still have a legal contract in every state. The result, if ever attempted, is a Pandora's box.

Here's why this kind of advice is horrible, aside from the money you may have just wasted (on the contracts and maybe the seminar). First, don't ask an attorney to "blend" *your* contract with the standard state form. As a lawyer for more than 16 years, I can tell you the worst contracts I've seen are ones that a nonlawyer has produced by cutting and pasting from contracts that he or she has found. Without knowing the origin of a contract, I can determine within a few seconds whether another lawyer or a layman produced it. The point should be obvious. If you cut your face and needed stitches and came to me to patch it up, a medical doctor or nurse practitioner would know in seconds that an untrained person had just butchered the job.

I learned quickly that I could produce my own contract faster than trying to "cut and paste" the clauses and text produced and requested by the client. Second, a lawyer does not want the liability of questionable text and clauses that the lawyer, or the lawyer's firm, has not produced. If your deal is complicated, you are better off just telling your lawyer what the specific terms of the deal are, and letting him or her handle it from there.

Here's the final kicker. This scenario is often pitched to save you money. The reasoning goes like this: your lawyer won't be able to charge you for a full contract, only for a simple revision. Poppycock. First, if you do what 99 percent of real estate investors do, you will use a standard contract produced by your state bar or board of Realtors. It will cost you *nothing*. If it's a big deal, a complicated deal, or a commercial transaction, let your attorney either review the standard form the broker has provided or use the form the attorney normally uses. You will save time, money, and the embarrassment of revealing to your legal advisor that you just came from "one of those seminars."

COMMON SEMINAR MISINFORMATION

Let me start, then, by addressing, and correcting, what is commonly taught and regurgitated at real estate seminars regarding real estate contracts. The following are the common statements.

"You need to use *our* contract, not the standard Realtor contract." Normally, this is said to entice you to buy real estate software, which includes contracts. Don't get me wrong, some of the real estate software that I've used is very good and worth every penny. However, you don't need the software for the contracts (the analysis and management modules are generally great). Long, specialized contracts are for purchasing very large *commercial* properties. If you attempt to purchase a residential property with a nonstandard (meaning not produced or approved by the bar or board of Realtors for your state) contract, the seller likely will see you as a flake. What's worse, if your offer is a bit low, that, combined with a "special" contract, will tell the seller that you are a real estate junkie who just came from a "get-rich-quick" real estate seminar. When you are negotiating, every red flag works against you. Don't start with one right out of the gate.

"Make sure you always put 'and/or assigns' after your name as the purchaser." The teaching goes that a seller really won't notice this and you can later assign this contract to someone else (as if everyone had two or three persons in line who would buy your deals and give you a finder's fee). This is more seminar hype. Whenever I hear this I assume that the speaker has never bought *any* real estate himself. Not ironically, you'll have trouble finding evidence that the guru actually purchased any investment property, even properties in what he claimed to be his niche.

Most people who attend real estate seminars have little money to use for buying real estate. As a result, the seminars pitch the notion that the attendees can make good money by just finding deals, getting them under contract, and assigning them to someone who does have money. Of course this is possible, but it's not an everyday occurrence. Most people who are broke don't rub shoulders at the country club with rich doctors, lawyers, developers, and business owners. But the training assumes that the beginner will start with assigning contracts because he or she has no money to work with. It sets up false expectations.

Back to the specific advice of adding "and/or assigns." First, most standard real estate contracts have *typeset* right into the form a section that specifies whether the contract may be assigned. You simply check one box or the other. In fact, following the seminar advice is once again counterproductive. By putting it into the top line, in handwritten or typewritten form, the addition draws dramatic attention to itself, much more than a small checked box on page two of a standard contract with very small typeset words and boxes.

Finally, making the contract assignable is one more red flag against you. The seller will begin to ask himself, "Why does he want to assign? Can't he close this deal? Is he for real? Can the assignee, who I don't know, close on the deal? Is he preapproved by a lender?"

The real estate guru usually has a ready-made rebuttal to a seller's objection. If the seller asks, "Why is this 'and/or assigns' in here?" the guru's ready answer is: "One of the reasons I have that in there is because I'm probably going to structure another corporation. With this addendum in there, that allows this contract to go in without writing out a new contract." He then reveals: "Did you notice how I started this out with 'one of the reasons . . .'? Obviously, you know that some of the other reasons include that you may assign it to someone else for cash."

In other words, the guru is suggesting that you lie to your seller. Certainly, such a practice is immoral. What's more, sellers quite often have a keen sense of radar for such subterfuge, and this kind of posturing will likely kill your deal. Unless you are planning to assign the contract, don't create a red flag. If you are planning to assign, check the box that deals with this rather than putting a spotlight on it at the top of the first page.

"Always give yourself an 'out' by adding, 'subject to partner approval' or 'subject to personal inspection'." Again, the advice is not only unnecessary, it is damaging. First, every real estate contract has "conditions precedent," which means conditions that have to be met for you to close. These conditions are: (1) your due diligence inspection/verification and (2) your financing.

Typically, a buyer has 30 days to close. After signing the contract, the buyer generally has about ten days to conduct a full inspection of the property and either present a repair list to the seller or walk from the deal. Between contract and close the buyer also has the right to get adequate records (i.e., rent roll, utility bills, etc.) from the seller. If your building fails your inspection, you walk. If the seller's records are inadequate, you walk. If your bank says the appraisal is less than the purchase price, you walk. These are standard conditions in every standard real estate form. If you write or type in "subject to partner approval," the seller will assume either: (1) You don't have the authority to be negotiating with him or her in the first place, or (2) you just came from one of "those seminars."

"Asking the seller to give you 100 percent financing is 'typically accepted 80 percent of the time'." This statement is not common but again confirms that the guru probably hasn't bought a single investment property. That quote is just not indicative of the real world. Sellers *sometimes* take back *some* paper (i.e., a second mortgage) or finance 80 percent of the purchase price (at best) when interest rates are high. But rates now are at 40-year lows. Sellers now will ask you, "Why do you need me to take back paper? You can get phenomenal conventional financing."

Sure, some sellers will take back notes for 10 to 20 percent of the purchase price to help close the deal (I've both taken back and given such paper), but to have a seller give you the keys and walk away with nothing from the closing table is highly unlikely. To say that 80 percent of sellers will do this is absurd.

You are far more likely to get 100 percent conventional financing on residential property (where one bank takes a first mortgage for 80 percent and a second bank takes a 20 percent second mortgage) than to get 100 percent seller financing. In fact, you would be quite lucky to have one seller in a hundred accept such an offer.

"Just put down $100 as an escrow deposit." Again, from the guru: "Deposit—put any amount in there, but make it at least $100. That's considered an appropriate exchange for real property. If you need to put more money down to make the deal, you can use a promissory note."

I recently purchased a triplex in Orlando for $370,000. On my initial offer, I put in the contract a $3,000 deposit. On the seller's counter, the seller's agent (apparently acting on his own) changed the deposit to $10,000. I asked the agent where he got that number from and he told me that 3 percent of the contract price was "normal." I assured him that it was not, and told him that I had just sold a property for $450,000 where the buyer put down only $2,000. I told him that it was always negotiable. I offered to increase the deposit to $6,000 and that was that. What do you think the seller's agent would have done had I put $100 on the deposit line of the contract?

Now, our guru suggests he is an expert in buying apartment complexes, which are commercial properties likely to start at $1.5 million and go up from there. Let's see, we'll make a serious offer with an escrow deposit of $100 to show the seller we're serious and credible. Right. "Oh, Mr. Seller, you need more than $100 to take your $1 million property off the market? No problem, I'll give you a promissory note for $20,000 to go along with my check." The sound you now hear will be laughter, followed by an escort to the front door.

But the guru isn't quite finished:

> Now, if a great deal comes up and the seller insists on more cash down than your standard $100, by all means consider and comply. My whole approach is speed. I tell sellers, "Look, if we do this quickly enough, the check won't even have time to clear in the escrow account before we close, so why even bother?"

I can sense that you are smiling. Good. If you've bought *any* real estate, even just a condo to live in, you know that residential closings normally take 30 days. Commercial properties can take 45 to 60 days. It takes a check two days to clear. Even if you had $1 million in your pocket you couldn't close in two days. Again, it's just more seminar mush to excite an audience and let them think they can get a property under contract for $100. In almost all cases, the seller will expect an escrow of at least one-half of 1 percent to 1 percent of the contract price. Anything less than that will be another red flag.

Contract extensions. Another suggested addendum from the guru:

> The Buyer has an unlimited number of extensions in lieu of x% of total purchase price to be applied to purchase price at closing.

Obviously, no seller with "all of the lights on" will let you tie up his or her property indefinitely. The fact that the buyer claims that he or she will pay for these extensions is meaningless. Who says the buyer has two nickels to rub together? With $100 in escrow, I'd assume the wannabe buyer is flat broke. Keeping a property off the market could cost the seller thousands, or tens of thousands, of dollars.

Closing dates are extended for two reasons. First, the closing agent (typically the title company or an attorney) is waiting on one or more documents (such as an appraisal) from the lender's underwriter or is booked up with closings. The delay should be for only a few days to a week. Second, in commercial settings, the buyer may request, and pay for, a second 30-day or 60-day "look" to complete his due diligence on the property. This could cost the buyer a flat nonrefundable fee, or it could just increase the purchase price a bit.

Don't shoot yourself in the foot with your offer. It's important to be as professional and credible as possible, particularly if you are negotiating a hard bargain. Use a standard form with standard addenda that the seller will expect. Get your own financing. Talk to a good mortgage banker. He or she can match you up with the right lender or lenders. If you stay with residential properties, you should be able to get excellent terms with 5 to 10 percent down. If necessary, your mortgage banker can probably get you 100 percent financing if you will live in the property. Follow these normal industry procedures and you'll have no problems getting your deals closed.

NEGOTIATION TIPS

Let's now talk about the important things that lead up to a contract, and some of the finer details of the contract itself. I have found the following points useful, if not imperative, in negotiating contracts as a lawyer and as a real estate investor. Because readers of this book will be both novice and experienced investors, I'll try to include everything.

Remember that everything is negotiable. Everything. That is, assuming the parties have equal, or almost equal, leverage. What people tend to forget is that negotiation is a game played with *leverage*. If a soccer game is played with 11 players against 5, the team with 11 players has a huge advantage. The same holds true with real estate negotiating, or any kind of negotiating for that matter.

As a lawyer, I was always negotiating with one hand tied behind my back if my client "had to have" that deal. My strongest negotiating tool for a buyer was always the option of walking. Sometimes that was my *only* tool. If you eliminate that from my arsenal, my leverage is gone.

Let's talk about leverage for a minute. As a buyer, if you don't "fall in love" with a property, and can walk away from it, you have the most leverage. Remember that. As a seller, if you have a nice property that is priced reasonably, you have a fair amount of leverage. If you live in the property or have it rented out, your leverage increases because you're in no hurry to get a buyer. Your expenses are covered.

However, if your property is vacant, your leverage drops dramatically. Both you and the buyer know that you have a big hole in your pocket. Everyone knows that you still have to make a mortgage payment and still have expenses, but you have no income from your property. You have become a "motivated seller." I have been on both sides of this equation and the leverage imbalance is quite obvious to everyone.

You increase your leverage by being able to walk away from the deal. Not long ago I put an offer on a property that I really liked. The sellers countered by coming off their original asking price just slightly. I countered back with what I thought was a very fair compromise. The sellers countered one more time and instructed their broker to say "This is our final offer." Now the *real* game was on. Who has the most leverage? I really wanted the property. The sellers wanted to sell, but assumed that they had the greatest leverage and so gave what amounted to an ultimatum— "Take it at this price or it's over."

Never give an ultimatum in negotiations. You may offend the other party and you surely will paint yourself into a corner. I didn't like what seemed to me to be arrogance—like the sellers were saying to me, "You want this property, we have the most leverage, so take it at this price or go away; no more discussions. Period." When I get that kind of response, I disappear. By doing so, I show the sellers that, in fact, they do not have the most leverage. I can buy another property.

My broker relayed what they had said—"Here's our final of-fer." I said, "Okay, just tell the other broker that their final offer is rejected." My broker said, "Anything else? Do you want to counter again?" I said, "No, just tell them exactly what I said—'Their final offer is rejected.'" My broker did so.

After about three days, the sellers' broker called my broker and said that the sellers *might* be willing to consider another counteroffer. In other words, the leverage game was still in play. My broker asked me if I wanted to put in another counter. I told him, "No, they told me theirs was a final offer." I did not put in another offer. The sellers lost the deal by bargaining too hard to squeeze out the last penny (we were only about $4,000 apart on a $435,000 property).

I moved on to another property. About a month later my bro-ker got a call from the sellers' broker. Turns out no one else put an offer in and they lowered the price. In fact, the sellers lowered the price *below* my second offer. For me, it was too late. For the sellers, it was a disastrous gamble to try to get a couple more thou-sand dollars out of the deal. The sellers lost.

Remember that unless the seller has a property that people are lining up to make an offer on, the buyer always has the ulti-mate leverage. If you are buying, remember that you can always walk from the deal and find another property.

SOME CONTRACT DETAILS

If you are using a broker and the standard real estate contract for your state, you'll avoid 85 percent of contract mistakes. Let me make a few comments on some selected sections, however.

Deposit. Try to put down an escrow deposit of 1 percent (or more) of the purchase price. If you go too much below that you'll lose some credibility. One suggestion that I do have is this:

I add "upon acceptance by Seller" at the end of the escrow deposit sentence. Much of the time a prospective buyer will give the deposit check with the offer. I don't like this idea for several reasons. First, if the seller's agent has the check, you don't know where it is going or if you'll get it back if the deal doesn't close. Even if it ends up being deposited by the agent in the broker's escrow account, how long will it take you to get it back? I don't like chasing my money.

Second, until the seller has signed the Purchase and Sale Agreement, you don't have a deal or commitment from the seller. As such, you don't need to commit your deposit either. Once the seller signs, your deposit goes in.

Third, I never give the seller's agent or broker my check. I don't even give *my* broker that check. I deposit my check with an independent law firm (my old law firm or with an attorney friend). I'll write in the name of this law firm in the contract section for "Escrow Agent." After the seller signs the contract, I drop off my check to the accounting person at the firm and he or she puts it in a client escrow account. There are very specific Bar rules on client escrow accounts so I know my money is safe there in case a dispute arises over the contract. I have never had a seller balk at my waiting for his or her signature to put up the deposit. Never.

Personal property conveyed. Just be sure to include all the appliances and other things that you want on this part of the form. On one investment property that I bought the seller had some nice but old antique furniture in the common area foyer. I listed the furniture in this section and they never objected. That came with the property, too.

Offer period. I generally give the seller two days to consider my offer. That's long enough so that the seller doesn't feel pressured, but short enough to keep the seller from "shopping the deal" (i.e., trying to get a better offer from another prospective buyer).

Closing date. If possible, I try to close on either the second, third, or fourth of the month to maximize my pro-rata rents. This means I try to put my offer in about 35 days out from this time frame. A seller will not want to wait 50 days just so you can close on a certain day. Sellers expect a 30-day time frame to close so work with that schedule.

Purchase price. I figure out what I think the real value of a property is. My initial offer will be somewhat lower than that, knowing that most sellers expect a little bargaining. I expect the seller to counter my offer, then I counter back, and we meet in the middle. I don't try to steal properties anymore. There are just too few out there to steal and you'll spend all your time looking for that needle in the haystack that you can get for $0.75 or $0.80 cents on the dollar.

Is it possible to find those bargains? Yes, I've done it. You can find them through "real estate owned" by banks (REOs), foreclosures, and tax deed sales. If the property is a disaster and needs tons of work (more than cosmetic), you can pick it up cheaply, too. But you better have good experience with this kind of rehab. Plus, these deals are hard to find, and it becomes depressing after a while when you can't find and close on all those bargains they promised you at the seminar you went to last month.

I generally try to get properties now at $0.90 to $0.95 on the dollar. That means I'm not trying to steal them. I'm paying a good price. I don't have to hide my head when I put in the offer. What I have as a priority above the sales price is a good, quality property in a great location. It goes back to your goal. If you are flipping properties to make a quick buck, you need to get them considerably under market value. That's not my approach, as mentioned in Chapter 2. I have a long-term plan for my properties.

I will make plenty of money over time using the strategies I've covered in this book. To get a *great* property, I'll pay 100 percent of the fair market value, or the asking price. Read Dr. Schumacher's book, *Buy and Hold,* sometime. He mentions that he'll pay *over* the fair market value if it's a great property in a great location. Over years, whether you bought a property at $0.80 or $1.10 on the dollar won't really matter. What is refreshing about this approach is that:

1. You don't have to look for "motivated" sellers.
2. You don't have to take advantage of anyone.
3. You don't have to be embarrassed by your offer.
4. You can expect to reach an agreement on just about all the deals you pursue.

If you find a good property in a good location, and you rehab it cosmetically, you don't need to look for the needle in the haystack or offend anyone. You'll make plenty of money and you'll be able to sleep at night as well.

11

CLOSING AND YOUR COSTS

Deals are my art form. Other people paint beautifully on canvas or write wonderful poetry.
I like making deals, preferably big deals.

—Donald Trump, *The Art of the Deal*

Many people approach a closing, at least their first one, with fear and trepidation. Primarily, this is because of the unknown—documents and fees. Most people have no idea what closing costs should be, or what they, as buyer or seller, are responsible for. I'll cover costs shortly.

First, who will be at the closing? Normally, the two parties, buyer and seller, and the closing agent (the title company or attorney). If brokers have been used, they will often come as well (usually to get their commission checks). My mortgage broker, Bob Baird, comes to my closings when I buy. He doesn't have to come, but he's a professional and wants to see that everything goes smoothly. Because he arranged the lender or lenders for me, he's also there for any last-minute questions I may have. He's the best in the business. These are the kinds of people you want on your team. Bob remembers the terms and structure of my deals better than I do, so he's always good to have around, or a phone call away. In fact, Bob helped me to provide the following numbers to assist you in your closings.

CLOSING COSTS

Buyer Costs

Closing costs are generally broken down into five different categories: lender fees, title charges, government fees, additional settlement charges, and prepaid expenses. For illustration purposes, I'll assume we're buying a $280,000 property with a $250,000 mortgage (which will determine costs for things such as documentary stamps). Let's take a look at each.

Lender fees. If you have agreed to pay points (one point equals 1 percent of the mortgage amount) or an origination fee, they would appear here. I never agree to those fees and these are not really "costs" per se, but are often used to get a better interest rate.

The most important lender cost will be the appraisal fee. For a house or duplex that expense might be $300 or $350. For a triplex or quad, your cost could go up to $450 or $550, depending on the size of your building and your market. You'll also find in this section the so-called "junk" fees. These include things such as "service preparation fee," "underwriting fee," and "tax service." The underwriting fee is often $400 and the preparation fee is often $200, while the tax fee is usually $75. These fees are simply "add-on" profit centers for your lender. They are not "hard costs," such as an appraisal (where your lender must pay an appraiser for a report), and sometimes can be negotiated away.

Together, these lender fees might add up to $1,450.

Title charges. Title charges should run about $350 in general fees. In addition, the buyer must pay for the lender's title policy, which will "piggyback" the owner's title policy, which the seller pays. The lender's policy should cost the buyer about $360. You also may be required to carry several endorsements to the policy, depending on the type of property (i.e., duplex, triplex, or quad). Count on another $100 to $300 here.

Factor in aggregate title charges of about $850.

Government and recording fees. Government and recording fees are set rates. The government fees are intangibles taxes and documentary stamps. In short, these fees are just more government taxes to create revenues for the county. In Florida, the buyer must pay an intangibles tax of .002 (times the loan amount) and documentary stamp taxes on the promissory note at .0035 (times the loan amount). In our example of a $250,000 loan, the intangibles tax would be $500, and the "doc stamps" tax would be $875. Recording fees will run about $1 per recorded page, and you can estimate 120 pages on average.

On our $250,000 note example, estimate costs of $1,495.

Additional settlement charges. The buyer is responsible for paying for the survey, which should run about $270 (in my area, at least).

Prepaid expenses. "Prepaids" and reserves are to set up an escrow account for taxes and insurance, which is required for all loans where the lender's loan-to-value (LTV) is more than 80 percent. You should expect your lender to escrow three months of property taxes if you are not putting 20 percent down. Property taxes normally run about 1.5 percent of the property's fair market value. Thus, on a $280,000 house, we'll pay about $4,200 per year, or $350 per month. Escrowing three months, then, would require a prepaid charge of $1,050.

You will also need to prepay one year of insurance coverage. Insurance annual premiums will be about $5 per $1,000 of property value, or 0.005 times value. If our house is worth $280,000, that's a prepaid of $1,400 ($280,000 × 0.005).

You also will pay daily interest on your loan for any closings before the month's end.

Accordingly, plan on prepaid expenses of $2,450, if taxes are escrowed, or $1,400 if they are not (not including interest charges, as noted).

THE TALLY

Using a property value of $280,000, and a loan amount of $250,000, your closing costs would typically be in the range of $5,465 to $6,515. Notice also that if you used a buyer-broker, with a listing commission of 6 percent, your 1.5 percent rebate (assuming you had a 50/50 split with your broker) of $4,200 would cover the majority of these costs. Add in prorated taxes and rents and you have more than covered all your closing costs.

Seller Costs

The seller is responsible for three things: broker commissions, owner's title insurance policy, and documentary stamps on the mortgage deed.

Real estate commissions. Broker commissions generally run from 5 to 7 percent for residential properties. Using an average of 6 percent in our sale of a $280,000 property, the seller would be paying $16,800 (with each broker typically receiving one-half).

Title charges. The seller is responsible for paying for an owner's title policy (to ensure you that the property conveys to you without encumbrances or clouds on the title). This fee will be determined by a promulgated rate for your area, which your title agent can give you.

Government fees. The seller is responsible for paying documentary stamps on the warranty deed (conveying title). This rate will be around .007 (times the sales price). On our $280,000 property, the seller would be charged $1,960.

Your lender is required by law to give you a "good-faith estimate" before closing to outline all these charges for you. If you have any questions, ask your mortgage broker (if you are using one) or your lender.

Part Three

HOLDING AND SELLING

12

MANAGING YOUR PROPERTY

I've owned and been renting property for 40 years, and I've never had any serious trouble with a tenant. You just have to know how to treat people.

—Dr. David Schumacher, *Buy and Hold*

I don't want to say much in this chapter because there's already great material available on property management. If you intend on owning income-producing property, you should read Leigh Robinson's classic, *Landlording* (Express, 2000). Let me make a few comments, however, about things Robinson does not address.

THE GENERAL PLAN

My general plan for owning residential multifamily property is to buy a triplex or quad (or duplex if the numbers work well), rehab it, and increase the rents. I prefer quads because you have more coverage during a vacancy. When one tenant moves out, you have three others covering your overhead costs. As each tenant moves out, you paint and clean that unit, and possibly put in a new appliance if necessary. At the same time, I do the cosmetics on the outside as well.

This formula improves the property, which leads to increased rents and better tenants. In my experience, rents are directly related to the quality of the tenants. The higher the rents, the better the tenants you will have. What does "better" mean? It means that they will pay their rent on time, will not throw wild parties at night, and will keep their units clean. Almost all my tenants have been exceedingly clean. They are generally very considerate and responsible.

A few years ago I was interested in purchasing 22 condos (a controlling interest) in a blue-collar complex just outside of Orlando. All the units were owned by one man, who controlled the condo association and rented out all his units. The area was lower middle class. It was not a slum. There was a decent-looking pool in the middle of the complex and the grounds were simple, but clean. In short, this was basic but safe housing. The numbers seemed to work well (they always do on the low end of the market), so I set an appointment to tour all 22 units for sale. I went during a weekday so almost all the tenants were at work.

What I saw as I toured each unit shocked me. These people lived like pigs. Of the 22 units, only one was nice and clean. A second was fairly normal. The rest were disastrous. Many units had open food on the dining room table, the kitchen counter, the stove, or in the sink. I could tell that people sat down the night before for dinner, ate, got up, and went to bed. The food and dishes stayed right where they were. It was an "all-you-can-eat" open buffet for roaches. I couldn't stomach that and vowed to stay away from low-income areas and properties. Some people can handle it. If so, great; the cash flow is excellent.

Ever since that time I've stayed with middle-class or upper-middle-class properties. The location of your property and the type of tenants already in place is a big part of this. For example, who rents a one-bedroom, one-bath apartment for $650? You could have a single, young professional right out of college or a family of four. If it's a family of four, there's a reason why they haven't purchased a house yet and cram four people into a small apartment. Which tenant will give you less headaches and wear and tear on your property?

Don't get me wrong. Everyone should have decent and safe housing. But unless you are getting Section 8 tenants and checks from the government every month, you should be selective about who you bring into your building. It is your building, after all, and you worked hard to get it. You will work hard to rehab it and make it nice.

People generally live where their peers live, even if the rents are the same someplace else. Personally, my preference for property locations is yuppie, downtown areas. These properties appreciate faster. They also draw good tenants. Naturally, my ideal tenants will be yuppies ("young, urban professionals" if it's been too long since you've seen that term). Part of the reason why young people flock to these areas is because they want to live downtown where it is fun, exciting, and close to work.

I meet this demand by advertising where only the young urban types will be looking—*http://www.craigslist.com*. Craig's List is a national site for finding housing, jobs, dates, personal effects (auto parts to jewelry), community activities, and chat rooms, all categorized by city. Just click on the city where you want to search, then under "housing" you'll see a number of sub-icons. Click on the first one, "apts/housing." This will give you a list of all the available apartments or houses for rent in that area, by date of entry. Many of these listings will provide a photo or several photos. So instead of running expensive ads in the local newspaper, which few young people read, I can place an ad here, with photos, free of charge. It doesn't get any better than that.

THE BEST WAY

The safest way to get involved in residential multifamily investing is to live in one of the units. If you are just getting started and don't have much money to work with, buy a duplex and live in one side and rent the other side. The best scenario is to buy a quad and live in one of the units. That's what I did. That's how Dr. David Schumacher started. The advantages are numerous. First, you get the best financing when it is an owner-occupied property. Second, you can claim a homestead exemption (because it is your personal residence) and lower your property taxes. Third, it is much easier to rehab the unit you live in, and the other units as they become vacant. Fourth, property management is much easier.

Let's talk about that last benefit. Some people don't want tenants to know that they own a property. They are afraid of the call in the middle of the night to fix a toilet. My response to that is: (1) If you choose good tenants, they won't call you at unreasonable times; (2) you *want* them to call you if the property has problems so you can protect your investment; and (3) you don't have to do any of the repairs yourself if you don't want to.

Have I received calls to fix things? Of course. Things wear out. Things happen in every property, even in very nice houses. Before I bought my quad I lived in a very nice, expensive home. We had a lightning storm one night and it zapped most of the houses on the street. I was fortunate. I only had to replace my electric garage door opener and two electrical outlets. Then there was the time rats got into the attic through a gap in the barrel tile roof. Even the best of properties will have problems. Count on it. But it's usually just a phone call to the right service company and the problem is solved.

I'm not very handy with repair things. Some of my tenant calls have been simple items that I could do (like replacing a toilet bowl flapper or shelving), while other calls have required a plumber or electrician. These are minor things when you look at the big picture. You are growing wealthy day by day. What's a call to a service person?

Most real estate books suggest not to get close to your tenants. Some even suggest lying to your tenants by telling them you are the property manager instead of the owner. I disagree. With the exception of one tenant (who I firmly believe had a "borderline personality" disorder), I've gotten along great with all my tenants. I became friends with a number of them. I've shared a beer with them, taken them to lunch, and patronized their places of employment. I give them gift certificates to places like Barnes & Noble at the end of the year. Aside from enjoying the friendship of another person, the additional benefit is that they will treat me, and my property, better.

If my tenants are a few days late on the rent, I don't freak out or charge them a late fee (even though my rental agreement allows it). I don't think anyone has paid rent later than the sixth of the month. In turn, they don't freak out if it takes me a while to fix a nonemergency item (like replacing a shelf). It just boils down to mutual respect and the golden rule—"Treat people the way you'd like to be treated."

I was pleased to read a similar position taken by Dr. Schumacher in his book, *Buy and Hold*. Dr. Schumacher has owned rental properties for more than 40 years and says he's never had a problem with a tenant. That's amazing when you think about it. How many tenants will you have over 40 years? And he's owned lots of four- and six-unit buildings. But he says basically what I'm saying here. He doesn't charge late fees. He doesn't hassle his tenants. He becomes friends with them and talks to them, getting to know them. Dr. Schumacher has forgotten more about property management than I'll ever know, so I think it's wise to hear what someone of his experience says.

SELECTING TENANTS

Choosing tenants is perhaps the most important part of your real estate career. A good tenant is worth his or her weight in gold. A bad tenant is a nightmare. Once again, I operate against traditional real estate advice. When screening for a tenant, I don't call employers. I don't call former landlords. I don't run Social Security numbers. Many landlords will be shocked to hear that. I don't know whether Dr. Schumacher does these things, but my guess is that he doesn't either.

How can I get great tenants without doing that? First, as I mentioned earlier, I don't operate in low-income housing. Sure, I know that people with money can be scam artists too (I foreclosed on one who I financed on a property). But more problems will arise as you move down the income ladder.

Second, and most important, I screen my tenants by talking to them, observing how they act, how they dress, and if they are on time for the appointment to see the unit they want. I look them in the eye. I look at their car. I also have them fill out my application, which asks for job and income information. Finally, I get a deposit equal to one month's rent. In the final analysis, I go with my "gut instincts." In my judgment, that's better than a call to some reference who could be the tenant's brother.

My instincts always seem to be right. The one bad tenant I had? It was my fault. I went against my judgment. I had a vacant unit and had a great tenant lined up. She was a local banker. Unfortunately, she had to back out at the last minute for some legitimate reason (job or boyfriend related). I was desperate for another renter. A kind of strange woman wanted to see the unit. She seemed to have some personal issues. She was a single mother and wanted to pay for six months rent up front (no discount). Seemed a bit odd but I said okay. When my assistant called to tell her she got the apartment, she cried.

Ironically, the banker called back the same day, but after I had told the other lady she could have the unit. The banker's conflict had worked out and she really liked the unit. She would have been a model tenant. But I felt morally obligated to go with the lady because I had just told her it was hers. As it turned out, this lady did have some serious emotional problems. She moved out one Sunday morning when I was gone, without notice, exactly at six months (she signed a year lease).

Other than that one tenant, I've always had great luck. And the people are often very different. I have one tenant now who has more tattoos on one arm than Cher and Angelina Jolie have on their combined bodies! But he's the nicest and most responsible guy. He's just a "free spirit." He's a musician (piano) and a waiter. He's waited on me as a customer in his restaurant. I really like him. He's going to be leaving soon to go to graduate school for music. I'll miss him.

So my best advice is to use your gut instincts when looking at prospective tenants. You have to make a quick judgment of character, but you can see a lot by how people act and speak, and where they work. If you make a mistake, you'll only have to deal with them for the length of your lease, if they don't leave before.

DEPOSITS

I normally require one month's rent as a security deposit. This is your only safety against a bad tenant, or a good tenant that has to leave for legitimate reasons. I have had a number of otherwise good tenants break their leases for job changes. They understand that they will lose their deposit, which covers you while you advertise for another tenant. A good tenant will give you plenty of advance notice if he or she has to break the lease, so you'll have at least one month, if not two or more, to get a new tenant.

RENTAL APPLICATIONS AND AGREEMENTS

Figure 12.1 is the rental application that I use. As you can see, it's very basic. I just want to know where the applicant works, and that he or she can afford the unit. While I normally do not run a credit check or call a previous landlord or employer, the information is there if I decide to. Getting that information also preserves the formality of the application.

Figures 12.2 and 12.3 are the basic rental agreements I use. Figure 12.2 is when the units are all on one utility meter, and Figure 12.3 is when there is a separate meter for each unit (see Paragraph 5). If the units are all on one meter, I apportion the utility expenses on a pro-rata basis.

STATE LAWS

Because state laws and local ordinances regarding tenancy differ, I debated whether to include my rental agreement here, which only applies to Florida. Your state may have specific laws regarding tenancy and may require statutory disclosures. For example, you will notice that Paragraph 22 mentions radon gas. This is a statutory (mandatory) disclosure in Florida. In addition, our state requires that any leases under seven months charge sales tax. As such, our leases are customarily for seven or twelve months.

Feel free to use the format or some of the provisions in my form. But find a good form from someone in your state that would include any statutory disclosures. If you don't have access to a landlord who will help you, real estate clubs in your area can assist you. In addition, you always can start with the form that your seller used. When you purchase a multifamily property that has tenants on existing leases, you must honor those leases. You have a ready-made form to use. You can edit it as you please for the next set of tenants.

FIGURE 12.1 *Application for Residency*

APPLICATION FOR RESIDENCY

APT. # _____

Personal Information:

Applicant's Full Name: _____

Social Security No.: _____

Driver's License No.: _____

Home Phone: _____   Work Phone: _____

Pager/Cell: _____   Emergency: _____

In Case Of Emergency, Notify: _____

Address: _____

Phone: _____   Relationship: _____

Residence History:

Present Address: _____

Community Name/Landlord: _____

Address: _____   Phone: _____

Monthly Payment: _____   Lease Expires: _____

Length Of Residence: _____ Years _____ Months

Reason For Moving: _____

Previous Address: _____

Community Name/Landlord: _____

Monthly Payment: _____

Reason For Moving: _____

Have You Ever Been Evicted From an Apartment or Broken Rental Agreement? _____

If So, Where? _____

Reason: _____

FIGURE 12.1   *Application for Residency (Continued)*

Employment Information:

Employer: _____   Phone: _____

Address: _____

Supervisor: _____   Position: _____

How Long: _____   Monthly Income: _____

Previous Employer: _____   Phone: _____

Address: _____

Position: _____   How Long? _____

Monthly Income: _____

Reason For Leaving: _____

Additional Information:

Auto Make/Model: _____   Year: _____   Color: _____

Tag No.: _____   State: _____

Applicant represents that all of the above statements are true and hereby authorizes verification of the above information, references, and credit records. Applicant acknowledges that false information herein may constitute grounds for rejection of this application.

Signature of Applicant: _____

Date: _____

One area that I'm a stickler with in nice units—I normally don't allow pets (Paragraph 14). They cause too much destruction. Some landlords don't mind pets and like the extra money that they get as a pet fee. But the smell that pets leave behind can be brutal and hard to eliminate.

I had a wonderful tenant once who found a feisty, barking dog running through the neighborhood. My tenant, a sweet girl with a tender spot for animals, figured that the dog was lost and she didn't want it to get hit by a car (even though the street is very quiet). The dog did not have an identification tag. My tenant knew that I didn't allow pets but she wanted to hold the dog and try to find the owner. I'm not sure if she took the dog into her unit that night, but first thing in the morning, I heard nonstop barking. It was the dog. She had tied him to the outside of the building with a two-foot extension cord and left for work! He was barking and going crazy, so I turned him loose. I left my tenant a note, reminding her about the "no pets" policy. As it turned out, my tenant did find the owner of the dog through craigslist.com! So it all worked out in the end.

You'll also note that I have a provision for a late fee (Paragraph 2). I never charge late fees, but I think you need to have such a provision, just in case you have a tenant who is repeatedly late in paying rent. It's also good that the tenants see you have the right, if you choose, to charge them if they are late in paying.

One thing I've found is that, if you have good tenants, you almost don't need a rental agreement. The agreement is for enforcing things if you have a bad tenant. Rent to a number of tenants over a period of time and your instincts will get better at knowing which ones could be trouble. Beyond that, let the golden rule be your guide.

RESIDENTIAL LEASE AGREEMENT

This Agreement is made this _____ day of _____ between _____ (herein referred to as "Landlord") and _____ (herein collectively referred to as "Tenant").

Property: _____ (sometimes referred to as the "Unit").

In consideration of the mutual covenants and agreements herein contained, Landlord hereby leases to Tenant and Tenant hereby leases from Landlord the above-described property under the following terms:

1. **Term:** This lease shall be for a term of _____ months, commencing _____ and ending _____ .

2. **Rent:** The rent shall be $_____ per month and shall be due on or before the first day of each month. Payments are late if they are not hand-delivered before 5 PM on the due date. Rent checks should be payable to _____ and be hand-delivered to _____ unless otherwise directed by Landlord. In the event the rent is received more than three (3) days late, a late charge of $25 shall be due, and $5 for each additional day until the rent is paid. This late charge can be deducted from the security deposit at the discretion of the Landlord. There shall be a $40 charge for each dishonored check (and late fees will owe if rent is late because check was dishonored for payment). Rent and late fees are to be paid without demand.

3. **Default.** In the event Tenant defaults under any terms of this lease, Landlord may recover possession as provided by law and seek monetary damages.

4. **Security Deposit.** Landlord acknowledges receipt of $_____ held as security deposit. In the event Tenant terminates the lease prior to its expiration date, or violates any provision under this Agreement, the entire security deposit shall be forfeited as a charge for Landlord's efforts in securing a new tenant, but Landlord reserves the right to seek additional damages if they exceed the security deposit.

5. **Utilities.** Tenant will be billed on a pro-rata share of the monthly utility expense, which includes electricity, gas, water, sewer, garbage, and trash, based upon the square footage of occupancy, or equal to _____ (_____ %) percent of the total monthly bill. That amount will be due and payable along with the monthly rent on the first day of the month. Tenant is to pay all other charges on the Unit, such as telephone and cable television.

6. **Maintenance.** Tenant has examined the property, acknowledges it to be in good repair and accepts its condition "as is." Tenant shall not keep or store water-filled furniture on the premises.

FIGURE 12.2 *Residential Lease Agreement (Pro-Rata Utilities) (Continued)*

The Unit shall be kept clean and free of garbage, trash, and debris. No condition shall be allowed to develop that would be unsightly or unsanitary; that would produce offensive odors; or would attract roaches, rodents, or other pests. Carpet shall be vacuumed frequently to prevent wear and damage from sand and grit. The Unit (especially tub and shower areas) shall be kept free of mildew and mold.

7. **Common Areas.** Tenant shall keep all common areas clean and clear of debris. Common areas shall include parking areas, lawn, porches, foyer, and laundry area. Tenant shall not use any common area for placement, storage, or temporary storage, for any items, including furniture, personal effects, or trash.

8. **Locks.** Tenant is prohibited from adding or changing locks on the premises. Landlord shall at all times have keys for access to the premises for inspection, pest control, maintenance, and in case of emergencies.

9. **Assignment.** Tenant may not assign this lease or sublet the Unit.

10. **Occupancy and Use.** Tenant shall not use the premises for any illegal or commercial purpose. Tenant shall not cause a nuisance for Landlord, neighbors, or other tenants. Such nuisance shall include, but not be limited to, excessive noise. The Unit shall be used exclusively as a residence for Tenant only. Guests staying for more than 14 days on one occasion, or more than 21 days in one year, will be deemed to be unauthorized occupants and such condition shall be a violation of this lease.

11. **Lawn.** Landlord will be responsible for all yard maintenance. Tenant shall not plant or place any outside plants or planters without the express permission of the Landlord.

12. **Liability.** Tenant shall be responsible for insurance on his or her own personal property and agree to hold the Landlord harmless for any damages whatsoever to Tenant's property or to any persons on said premises.

13. **Access.** Landlord reserves the right to enter the Unit for the purposes of inspection, maintenance, pest control, and to show the Unit to prospective purchasers or tenants.

14. **Pets.** Pets of any kind are not permitted on the premises.

15. **Parking.** Parking for Unit _____ shall be _____ . Vehicles not in operating condition, commercial vehicles, or motorcycles shall not be parked or stored on the premises or the street.

16. **Alterations.** Tenant shall not make any alterations to the property without the written consent of the Landlord, and any such alterations or improvements shall become the property of the Landlord. Alterations include, but are not limited to, painting, window coverings, and lighting fixtures.

17. **Smoke Detectors.** Tenant shall be responsible for keeping smoke detectors operational and/or changing the battery when and as needed.

18. **Repairs.** Landlord shall repair and maintain the premises, including, but not limited to, air-conditioning and heating units, ductwork, appliances, electrical fixtures, roof, and foundation, except damage caused by the intentional or negligent acts of Tenant or Tenant's guests or invitees. Tenant shall promptly give notice by phone or in writing to Landlord of any repairs or maintenance needed, and shall take all reasonable measures to protect the premises from any further damage until such repairs can be made. The Landlord shall cause such repair or maintenance to be performed at Landlord's expense within 30 days upon receipt of said notice. Tenant shall indemnify and hold Landlord harmless from and against any and all liability from any damage, injury, or claim whatsoever arising from any defect, hazard, dangerous condition, need for repair or maintenance, whether or not known to or caused by Landlord, unless the foregoing notice provision has been strictly complied with. Tenant is wholly responsible for the cost of the following repairs: (1) repair of Tenant-caused damages; (2) replacement of broken glass; (3) repair of ripped screens; (4) unstopping drains when blockage is Tenant-caused; (5) repair of excess damages caused by Tenant's failure to promptly notify Landlord of need for repair; (6) damage caused by Tenant's failure to take reasonable measures to protect the premises until repairs could be made. Nonemergency repairs shall be made during normal business hours. If Tenant chooses to have repairs made after hours or on weekends or holidays for Tenant's comfort or convenience, the Tenant shall pay any premium charged. Note: Air-conditioning is considered a "nonemergency" repair.

19. **Surrender of Premises.** At the expiration of the terms of this lease, Tenant shall immediately surrender the premises in the same clean condition as existed at the start of the lease. "Clean" means bathroom scoured, carpet shampooed, floors mopped, walls clean, kitchen appliances clean, and otherwise suitable for immediate occupancy. If the premises are not vacated in "clean" condition, the cost of returning the unit to its "clean" condition will be deducted from the security deposit.

20. **Vacancy and Cleaning.** Upon vacancy of the Unit, Tenant is responsible for leaving the Unit in the same condition as when Tenant commenced the lease. If the Unit is not clean and otherwise in the same condition as when Tenant commenced the lease, Landlord may charge a $75 cleaning fee, which will be deducted from the security deposit.

21. **Abandonment.** In the event Tenant abandons the Unit prior to the expiration of the lease, Landlord may relet the premises and hold Tenant liable for any costs, lost rent, or damage to the Unit or premises. Landlord may dispose of any property abandoned by Tenant.

22. **Radon Gas.** Radon is a naturally occurring radioactive gas that, when it has accumulated in a building in sufficient quantities, may present health risks to persons who are exposed to it over

FIGURE 12.2 *Residential Lease Agreement (Pro-Rata Utilities) (Continued)*

time. Levels of radon that exceed federal and state guidelines have been found in buildings in Florida. Additional information regarding radon and radon testing may be obtained from your county public health unit.

23. **Waiver.** Any failure by Landlord to exercise any rights under this Agreement shall not constitute a waiver of Landlord's rights.

24. **Severability.** In the event any section of this Agreement shall be held to be invalid, all remaining provisions shall remain in full force and effect.

25. **Attorney's Fees.** In the event it becomes necessary to enforce this Agreement through the services of an attorney, tenant shall be required to pay Landlord's attorney's fees.

26. **Entire Agreement.** This lease constitutes the entire agreement between the parties and may not be modified except in writing signed by both parties.

Witness the hands and seals of the parties hereto as of the day first above written.

Landlord: Tenant:

_____   _____

FIGURE 12.3 *Residential Lease Agreement (Separate Utilities)*

RESIDENTIAL LEASE AGREEMENT

This Agreement is made this _____ day of _____ between _____ (herein referred to as "Landlord") and _____ (herein collectively referred to as "Tenant").

Property: _____ (sometimes referred to as the "Unit").

In consideration of the mutual covenants and agreements herein contained, Landlord hereby leases to Tenant and Tenant hereby leases from Landlord the above-described property under the following terms:

1. **Term:** This lease shall be for a term of _____ months, commencing _____ and ending _____ .

2. **Rent:** The rent shall be $_____ per month and shall be due on or before the first day of each month. Payments are late if they are not hand-delivered before 5 PM on the due date. Rent checks should be payable to _____ and be hand-delivered to _____ unless otherwise directed by Landlord. In the event the rent is received more than three (3) days late, a late charge of $25 shall be due, and $5 for each additional day until the rent is paid. This late charge can be deducted from the security deposit at the discretion of the Landlord. There shall be a $40 charge for each dishonored check (and late fees will owe if rent is late because check was dishonored for payment). Rent and late fees are to be paid without demand.

3. **Default.** In the event Tenant defaults under any terms of this lease, Landlord may recover possession as provided by law and seek monetary damages.

4. **Security Deposit.** Landlord acknowledges receipt of $_____ held as security deposit. In the event Tenant terminates the lease prior to its expiration date, or violates any provision under this Agreement, the entire security deposit shall be forfeited as a charge for Landlord's efforts in securing a new tenant, but Landlord reserves the right to seek additional damages if they exceed the security deposit.

5. **Utilities.** Tenant shall be responsible for the monthly utility expenses, which includes electricity, gas, water, sewer, and trash collection. Tenant also is responsible for all other charges on the Unit, such as telephone and cable service.

6. **Maintenance.** Tenant has examined the property, acknowledges it to be in good repair and accepts its condition "as is." Tenant shall not keep or store water-filled furniture on the premises. The Unit shall be kept clean and free of garbage, trash, and debris. No condition shall be allowed to develop that would be unsightly or unsanitary; that would produce offensive odors; or would

FIGURE 12.3 *Residential Lease Agreement (Separate Utilities) (Continued)*

attract roaches, rodents, or other pests. Carpet shall be vacuumed frequently to prevent wear and damage from sand and grit. The Unit (especially tub and shower areas) shall be kept free of mildew and mold.

7. **Common Areas.** Tenant shall keep all common areas clean and clear of debris. Common areas shall include parking areas, lawn, porches, foyer, and laundry area. Tenant shall not use any common area for placement, storage, or temporary storage, for any items, including furniture, personal effects, or trash.

8. **Locks.** Tenant is prohibited from adding or changing locks on the premises. Landlord shall at all times have keys for access to the premises for inspection, pest control, maintenance, and in case of emergencies.

9. **Assignment.** Tenant may not assign this lease or sublet the Unit.

10. **Occupancy and Use.** Tenant shall not use the premises for any illegal or commercial purpose. Tenant shall not cause a nuisance for Landlord, neighbors, or other tenants. Such nuisance shall include, but not be limited to, excessive noise. The Unit shall be used exclusively as a residence for Tenant only. Guests staying for more than 14 days on one occasion, or more than 21 days in one year, will be deemed to be unauthorized occupants and such condition shall be a violation of this lease.

11. **Lawn.** Landlord will be responsible for all yard maintenance. Tenant shall not plant or place any outside plants or planters without the express permission of the Landlord.

12. **Liability.** Tenant shall be responsible for insurance on his or her own personal property and agree to hold the Landlord harmless for any damages whatsoever to Tenant's property or to any persons on said premises.

13. **Access.** Landlord reserves the right to enter the Unit for the purposes of inspection, maintenance, pest control, and to show the Unit to prospective purchasers or tenants.

14. **Pets.** Pets of any kind are not permitted on the premises.

15. **Parking.** Parking for Unit _____ shall be _____ . Vehicles not in operating condition, commercial vehicles, or motorcycles shall not be parked or stored on the premises or the street.

16. **Alterations.** Tenant shall not make any alterations to the property without the written consent of the Landlord, and any such alterations or improvements shall become the property of the Landlord. Alterations include, but are not limited to, painting, window coverings, and lighting fixtures.

17. **Smoke Detectors.** Tenant shall be responsible for keeping smoke detectors operational and/or changing the battery when and as needed.

FIGURE 12.3   *Residential Lease Agreement (Separate Utilities) (Continued)*

18. **Repairs.** Landlord shall repair and maintain the premises, including, but not limited to, air-conditioning and heating units, ductwork, appliances, electrical fixtures, roof, and foundation, except damage caused by the intentional or negligent acts of Tenant or Tenant's guests or invitees. Tenant shall promptly give notice by phone or in writing to Landlord of any repairs or maintenance needed, and shall take all reasonable measures to protect the premises from any further damage until such repairs can be made. The Landlord shall cause such repair or maintenance to be performed at Landlord's expense within 30 days upon receipt of said notice. Tenant shall indemnify and hold Landlord harmless from and against any and all liability from any damage, injury, or claim whatsoever arising from any defect, hazard, dangerous condition, need for repair or maintenance, whether or not known to or caused by Landlord, unless the foregoing notice provision has been strictly complied with. Tenant is wholly responsible for the cost of the following repairs: (1) repair of Tenant-caused damages; (2) replacement of broken glass; (3) repair of ripped screens; (4) unstopping drains when blockage is Tenant-caused; (5) repair of excess damages caused by Tenant's failure to promptly notify Landlord of need for repair; (6) damage caused by Tenant's failure to take reasonable measures to protect the premises until repairs could be made. Nonemergency repairs shall be made during normal business hours. If Tenant chooses to have repairs made after hours or on weekends or holidays for Tenant's comfort or convenience, the Tenant shall pay any premium charged. Note: Air-conditioning is considered a "nonemergency" repair.

19. **Surrender of Premises.** At the expiration of the terms of this lease, Tenant shall immediately surrender the premises in the same clean condition as existed at the start of the lease. "Clean" means bathroom scoured, carpet shampooed, floors mopped, walls clean, kitchen appliances clean, and otherwise suitable for immediate occupancy. If the premises are not vacated in "clean" condition, the cost of returning the unit to its "clean" condition will be deducted from the security deposit.

20. **Vacancy and Cleaning.** Upon vacancy of the Unit, Tenant is responsible for leaving the Unit in the same condition as when Tenant commenced the lease. If the Unit is not clean and otherwise in the same condition as when Tenant commenced the lease, Landlord may charge a $75 cleaning fee, which will be deducted from the security deposit.

21. **Abandonment.** In the event Tenant abandons the Unit prior to the expiration of the lease, Landlord may relet the premises and hold Tenant liable for any costs, lost rent, or damage to the Unit or premises. Landlord may dispose of any property abandoned by Tenant.

22. **Radon Gas.** Radon is a naturally occurring radioactive gas that, when it has accumulated in a building in sufficient quantities, may present health risks to persons who are exposed to it over time. Levels of radon that exceed federal and state guidelines have been found in buildings in Florida. Additional information regarding radon and radon testing may be obtained from your county public health unit.

FIGURE 12.3 *Residential Lease Agreement (Separate Utilities) (Continued)*

23. **Waiver.** Any failure by Landlord to exercise any rights under this Agreement shall not constitute a waiver of Landlord's rights.

24. **Severability.** In the event any section of this Agreement shall be held to be invalid, all remaining provisions shall remain in full force and effect.

25. **Attorney's Fees.** In the event it becomes necessary to enforce this Agreement through the services of an attorney, tenant shall be required to pay Landlord's attorney's fees.

26. **Entire Agreement.** This lease constitutes the entire agreement between the parties and may not be modified except in writing signed by both parties.

Witness the hands and seals of the parties hereto as of the day first above written.

Landlord: Tenant:

_____   _____

13

HOW TO SELL AND PAY NO TAXES

The hardest thing in the world to understand is the income tax.

—Albert Einstein

As a real estate investor, you should know about five major tax regulations applicable to income properties. First, you should know about depreciation, which I covered in Chapter 4. Second you should know about three rules that may apply when selling your property, which I introduced in Chapter 4:

1. Capital gains tax
2. 1031 exchange
3. Personal residence exemption

Knowing and applying these three rules will save you tens of thousands of dollars. Finally, if you live in your property, you should file for a homestead exemption to lower your property taxes. Let's look at each rule in more detail.

CAPITAL GAINS TAX

When you sell your property you'll soon realize that you had a silent partner on the investment—Uncle Sam. The government wants a piece of the profit action. You have two scenarios.

If you hold the property for under one year and sell it, your capital gains (the difference between your acquisition costs and improvements and the selling price) will be taxed as ordinary income. This means you will be taxed at your income bracket level (i.e., 28 percent or 33 percent). So if you purchased a property in January for $180,000 and had $15,000 in closing and rehab costs, your "basis" would be $195,000. Suppose you sold it in June for $245,000. Your capital gains would be $50,000. Let's take a look.

Purchase price	$180,000
Costs and improvements	+ 15,000
Basis	$195,000
Sales price	$245,000
Less basis	− 195,000
Capital gains ("profit")	$50,000

Because you held this property for less than one year, your gains would be taxed as ordinary income. Assume you are in the 33 percent tax bracket. You would pay Uncle Sam $16,500 in taxes so that your net is $33,500. This is one of the disadvantages of flipping properties. Your "silent partner" gets a big piece of the pie.

Let's assume now that you held the property over one year. Now you qualify for long-term capital gains treatment. Thus, you are not taxed according to your income bracket, but at a flat rate of 15 percent. Compare the difference.

	Held under one year	Held over one year
Treatment:	Ordinary income	Long-term capital gains
Tax rate:	33%	15%
Taxes paid:	$16,500	$7,500
Net profit:	$33,500	$42,500

By holding a few extra months, you save $9,000 in taxes. But what if your gain was $500,000, instead of $50,000? If so, you would save $90,000. It makes a big difference. Why not wait one full year?

1031 EXCHANGE

There is a way to *delay* paying taxes, perhaps for 20 or 30 years, on that last transaction. Suppose you made $500,000 on a property sale. Do you want to pay Uncle Sam $90,000 of that? I didn't think so. Most investors delay paying that tax by using the IRS's 1031 exchange rule.

The 1031 exchange allows an investor to roll all of his or her net proceeds into another investment property without paying tax at that time. The gain is preserved, to be taxed later if you sell the next property without using the 1031 exchange again. But when you sell the second property you can use 1031 again, and again defer taxes. This "exchanging" process can go in indefinitely. There are numerous rules that apply, but they are easy to work with. Here's what you must do to qualify for a 1031 exchange.

1. When you sell your property you must give all your net proceeds to a *1031 exchange agent* to hold in escrow. This agent must be independent, and could be a title or escrow company, or a bank. However, your attorney, accountant, and broker are not considered "independent." In addition, your agent must hold *all* your net proceeds. You cannot take any part of your profit, or "boot," for personal use.

2. *You must notify your agent, within 45 days of your closing, of a target acquisition property (your "exchange" property).* You may give your agent up to three target properties.

3. *Your acquisition target property must be of a "like kind."* In other words, it also must be an income-producing property, but not necessarily the exact same kind. For example, you could have sold an apartment building on the first sale, but invested in an office building or shopping center on the second deal.

4. *You must close on one of your target properties within 180 days from your first property closing.*

5. *You must apply 100 percent of your escrowed proceeds to that second property* (you cannot take any money out for personal use).

Can you see the phenomenal benefit of this tax rule? Let's say your first property netted you $50,000. You then invest this in a $500,000 property with the $50,000 proceeds as your down payment, following the 1031 rules. Three years later you sell that property for a $150,000 gain. You roll that gain, plus your $50,000 down payment, or $200,000, into your third property. Perhaps this was a $1 million property on which you put 20 percent down. Three years after that you sell this property for a $300,000 gain. Taking that, plus your $200,000 down payment, you now roll $500,000 into a $2.5 million property. And on it goes. You keep "trading up," or pyramiding your equity into bigger properties. In essence, Uncle Sam is letting you use his tax money to invest for Uncle Sam, interest-free. Your uncle isn't so bad after all.

PERSONAL RESIDENCE EXEMPTION

Uncle Sam is going to do you another favor if you will live in your investment property. Again, remember that 2–4 unit properties are considered residential in nature. As such, even though you may be in a quad, renting out the other three units, you are treated by lenders (for financing purposes) and the IRS (for personal residence tax breaks) as if it were a single-family home.

Here's the current tax law regarding personal residences: If you live in your house (or duplex, triplex, or quad) for at least two years, you can pocket any gain on resale, up to certain amounts, *tax-free*. Here's the technical rule: You must have

- owned the home for at least two of the past five years (ownership test), and
- you must have lived there as your main residence for at least two years (use test).

If you are single, you can pocket the first $250,000 gain tax-free. If you are married and filing jointly, you can pocket the first $500,000 tax-free if all of the following are also true:

- Either you or your spouse meets the ownership test.
- Both you and your spouse meet the use test.
- Neither you nor your spouse used the exemption in the past two years.

If you need to "catch up" in your financial life, this is a great way to do it. And the best part is, you can do it every two years! This is exactly what I'm doing. As I write this, I have one more month to reach my two-year threshold on the quad that I live in. If I decide to sell my property in the near future, my gain upon sale will be much greater than $250,000, but the first quarter million will go in my pocket, tax-free. I can now use 100 percent of that money to buy several quads. Just using my tax-free money, I can purchase $2.5 million in residential properties, using 10 percent down. My guess is that this tax benefit won't be around forever. Use it while it's here!

HOMESTEAD EXEMPTION

While the other tax regulations apply to federal income taxes, this tax rule applies to local (i.e., county) property taxes. In virtually every state, an owner who lives in a property as his or her primary residence may file for a homestead exemption. By filing for this exemption, the owner's property taxes will be reduced. In my state (Florida), the valuation of a property (the county's tax-assessed value) will be reduced by 25 percent if it is a homestead. That discount is real, substantial, and automatic with the filing.

Again, it doesn't matter that you have an income-producing property. As long as it is four units or less, it is classified as residential property. If you live in one of the units as your primary residence, you qualify for the homestead exemption. No other form of real estate investing offers this generous benefit.

YOUR WEALTH-BUILDING PROGRAM

14

THE FASTEST *AND* SAFEST
WAY TO WEALTH

Dishonest money dwindles away, but he who gathers money little by little makes it grow.

—Proverbs 13:11

If you've been reading this book carefully, you'll see the power of combining benefits, especially if you live in your property for two years or more. If you will plan out a two-year strategy, you can set yourself up for financial freedom and wealth-building right now. You only have to do it once. This is exactly what I did to take advantage of all the benefits offered by residential multifamily property investing. I call this the "Wealth-Building Foundation Plan":

1. Buy a residential multifamily (2–4 unit) property.
2. *Put 0 to 10 percent* down and get the best lending rates.
3. *Live in one unit while rehabbing the other units.*
4. *File for a homestead exemption* with your county to get a sizable reduction in your property taxes (25 percent reduction in your assessed value in Florida).
5. *Live rent-free.* If you buy a triplex or quad, your other renters should cover your expenses.

6. *Raise the rents* as each unit is rehabbed.

7. *Refinance after one year* to pull out cash to buy another property. The cash you pull out is *tax-free* (because it's loan money).

8. *Sell the property you live in (if you want) after two years.* Your profits (capital gains) will be *tax-free* (up to the limits). Otherwise, refinance the property to free up more cash to buy again.

9. Repeat the process.

Show me another real estate investment strategy where you can

- put little or nothing down,
- live rent-free,
- get a homestead exemption,
- receive tax-free money to buy a second property,
- actually get to *write off* that tax-free money (the interest is deductible), and
- sell your first property and pocket the profits, tax-free.

If you think this is too good to be true, it is not. I have done it. Follow my history:

- I bought a $390,000 quad (Property #1) with 100 percent financing.
- I live rent-free.
- I have a homestead exemption.
- I refinanced after one year and bought a $392,000 property (Property #2) with *part* of the proceeds.
- I get to write off the proceeds I used to buy the second property because it's loan money.
- My appraised value on Property 1 was $520,000 after one year (equity gain of $130,000).

- My appraisal value on Property #1 was $615,000 after 22 months (equity gain of $225,000). The property is worth much more than that now based on market conditions. I can sell the quad after two years and pocket the first $250,000, tax-free.
- I purchased Property #3 (a triplex), primarily using proceeds left over from the refi on Property #1.

Remember that I started the process with *nothing down*. Where else can you do this? I don't think there's been another time in our history (or anyplace else in the world) where we have extremely low interest rates (making your mortgage payments affordable), ease of financing, preferential treatment for residential multifamily housing, and the ability to pocket a small fortune, tax-free. As they say in the country, "If this doesn't light your fire, your wood's wet!"

GETTING STARTED

At this point, you probably have a good idea of where you want to start. I hope I've convinced you that residential multifamily property investing is the fastest and safest way to real estate wealth. However, everyone is different. Some people have money but little time. Others have time, but no money. Some people have both, but need a big change over the next 10 or 15 years. I'm going to lay out two plans. Figure out which plan works best for you. If you don't fit perfectly into one of these, mix them to fit your needs.

THE "SAFE AND EASY" PLAN

This plan is for those people who have some money to work with, have a long-range perspective (20 years or more), and don't really want to be inconvenienced by living in a multifamily property they own. Here's your strategy:

1. *Buy a quad.* The numbers simply work best with more units. If you have the cash, buy several quads.
2. *Put 10 percent down.* That should be enough to keep you in positive cash flow (or close to it, depending on your market), but not so much to kill your return on investment.
3. *Use a buyer who knows the market and invests in multifamily properties as well.*
4. *Buy in high-appreciation areas.* You may pay a bit of a premium for them, and you might even have negative cash flow for a year or so, but the appreciation will more than compensate.
5. *Rehab and increase the rents as fast as possible.*
6. *Never sell before one year.* This way you'll qualify for long-term capital gains treatment when you do sell.
7. *Refinance after one year and buy a second property.*
8. *Watch the GRM range* in your area so you know the going prices when you buy. If you decide to sell and your neighborhood is on the upswing, you'll get a tremendous windfall, especially after raising the rents.
9. *If you sell, buy another quad with a 1031 Exchange,* using the proceeds from the sale of your first property (if you didn't "refi and buy"). This way, you will be able to roll 100 percent of your capital gains into the next property.
10. *Keep putting 10 percent down* (or more if you need to avoid negative cash flow) until you run out of quads or triplexes to buy. Eventually, you may need to move to more units.
11. When you reach the point where you must go to larger units, perhaps a 10- to 15-unit building, put 20 percent down, rehab, raise the rents, and continue to *pyramid up.*

By your third or fourth cycle of doing this, you will be financially set for life.

THE BOOTSTRAP PLAN

Use this plan if you are flat broke, if you need to set up yourself for retirement quickly, or if you just want to maximize your investments. This plan has the most benefits and the highest ROI. If you like real estate like I do, this plan is also the most fun because you have more "chess players" to use in the game. Each "player," or technique, either gives you money or saves you money. I think it's fun to use all the players on the board, so to speak.

1. *Use a buyer-broker, where available.* If you don't, you are leaving a fair amount of money on the table. Remember that broker commissions run from 5 to 7 percent, and that commissions are split between the two brokers. Thus, if the listing commission was 6 percent, you would receive one-half of your broker's 3 percent commission, or 0.015 of the sales price. This will give you thousands of dollars from the outset.

2. *Find a good mortgage broker.* They are worth their weight in gold. Your mortgage broker can match your needs to the right lender and get the best rates. Some people have little cash and need to find 100 percent financing. Others are self-employed or otherwise need a "stated income" qualification. Some people have great credit and some have bad credit. Your mortgage broker can find what you need. I use the same mortgage broker on every property I buy. He's the best and looks out for my best interest, not for how much money he can make.

3. If possible, *buy a triplex or quad* to increase your safety and cash flow.

4. *Close on the second or third of the month.* This also will give you thousands of dollars from the get-go. If you will use a buyer-broker and close on the second or third (no mortgage payment this month), you will cover your closing costs and have money available for rehab.

5. *Put down 0 to 5 percent.* If you have little money, you can get 100 percent financing. If you do this, your mortgage rate will not be quite so good, but it will be close to a 5 percent down scenario. If you put 5 percent down, your rate will be a bit better, and your payment will be slightly less. Just analyze the numbers carefully to make sure that you won't have negative cash flow, or that you can cover it until you can rehab and raise the rents. If you are a veteran, you also can get 100 percent financing through a VA loan.

6. *Lower your payment with interest-only or adjustable loans.* The problem with 100 percent financing is that it makes it very difficult to cash-flow the property. You can overcome that hurdle usually by having an interest-only or adjustable rate mortgage (ARM), which has low interest rates with substantially lower payments. This strategy increases your risk, of course, so you need to look at the deal, the numbers, the rents, the occupancy, the rehab costs, the new rents, and such other factors very carefully. Using an interest-only or ARM loan should bootstrap you into that first property. When you refinance in a year, you can change it to a conventional mortgage if you want. Right now, we're trying to get you into the game. Talk to your mortgage broker about these options.

7. *Close later in the year to capture prorated taxes.* You know that the rents are prorated. So are the property taxes. Generally, property taxes will run about 1½ percent of the fair market value of the property. On a $250,000 property, that's $3,750 in taxes annually, or $312.50 per month.

The taxes are paid in arrears. That is, you will be required to pay in January or February the taxes for the prior year.

Now suppose that you decide to buy this property on March 1. For the current year, property taxes have accrued for two months, January and February. But these taxes have not been paid because they are not yet due. The bill will not come for another 11 months. As the new owner, you will be responsible for the taxes for those two months, even though you did not own the property then. As such, the closing agent will give you a credit on the closing statement for $625, or the taxes that the seller owes you. That's $625 less you need to bring to the closing table.

Now what if you were closing on August 1? The seller now will owe you taxes for seven months, or $2,187.50. So you'll get a credit at closing for this amount. That's a sizable chunk of change. You will be responsible for that tax bill, of course, but it won't be due until January or February, after you've had a chance to rehab and maybe increase the rents.

If you don't have a lot of money to start with, let's look at what you've brought to the closing table thus far, assuming our $250,000 purchase:

- *Buyer-broker.* If the commission in your area is 6 percent and the listing has the typical equal split between brokers, you should get half of your broker's commission, or $3,750. Some buyer-brokers will not give you quite half of their commission, so keep searching until you find one who does.
- *Prorated rents.* Let's assume you are purchasing a triplex that has monthly rents of $600, or $1,800 per month total. If you close on the second of the month in a month with 30 days, you get 29/30ths of that amount, or $1,740.

- *Security deposits.* If your deposits equal the rents, that's $1,800. Granted, you know this is not your money, but you still get a credit for it at the closing table.
- *Prorated taxes.* Assuming that you closed on August 1, you'll get a credit of about $2,187.50. These taxes will be due in six or seven months.

Let's tally up what you've just brought to the closing table:

Buyer-broker rebate	$3,750
Prorated rents	1,740
Security deposits	1,800
Prorated taxes	2,187
Total	$9,477

Your closing costs will vary, depending on a number of factors, but should be around $5,000. If you financed the deal 100 percent, you would bring nothing to the table, and would walk away from closing with $4,477. Your state may require you to put the $1,800 in deposits in a separate account, but the rest of that money can be used for rehab. You won't find this kind of windfall in any other type of investing, real estate or otherwise.

8. *Move into one of the units.* Remember, you are trying to capture every possible benefit. By moving into your property, your mortgage will be based on an "owner-occupied" status and afford you better rates. Because it is your residence, you can, and should, file for a homestead exemption to lower your property taxes.

When I did this, I moved into the best unit, which previously drew the highest rents. If you are hurting for cash, however, you should move into the cheapest renting unit to maximize your cash flow. Dr. David Schumacher did exactly that on the first property he bought. After you are financially stable, you can always move to one of the better units as tenants move out.

9. *Rehab as you go.* The good thing about following this plan is that you don't have to do all of the rehab at once. That would be both a time and a financial burden. However, by following the plan I'm outlining, you can do a little as you go. For example, if the building is fully occupied, just work on the outside. Do your exterior painting and the landscaping. Clear away excess brush or leaves. Paint the porch and railings. You may want to pressure-clean the driveway and sidewalk (if you have one). When the first tenant leaves, you could move into that unit and begin painting and cleaning it. When the second tenant leaves, you jump on that one, and so on. By working on one section at a time, it makes it more manageable and less stressful.

10. *Raise the rents.* After you rehab the outside of the property and the inside of each unit, raise the rents to the market for a similarly located, equally nice property. It's crucial that you know what the rents are in your area. Because you are valuing the property on the basis of the gross rents multiplier (GRM), you want to squeeze every dollar you can out of each unit, without going over the market price.

11. *Refinance in one year and buy a second property.* After owning the property for one year, you are eligible for a new appraisal and refinancing. If you have rehabbed both the outside and the inside of your property, and raised your rents, you will have a nice equity foundation to work with.

Generally, a lender will allow you to pull out equity up to an 80 percent LTV of the new appraisal. However, as you saw in the analysis of my own recent deal in Chapter 5, you may be able to go up to 90 percent of a CLTV (combined loan-to-value) with a second lender. By having access to this much of your equity, you'll have plenty of cash to work with to buy another property.

12. *Work the same plan on your new (second) property.*

13. *In the second year of ownership, you may want to look into getting a home equity line of credit (you can only refinance once a year) if you have the equity to make it worthwhile. If so, buy again.*

14. *If you need to sell the property that you are living in, make sure you sell it after year two of ownership so that you can pocket the proceeds, tax-free.* As you saw in Chapter 13, if you live in a property as your personal residence for two years, a single person can pocket the first $250,000 in gain (a married couple up to $500,000), tax-free.

15. *Buy a third (or fourth) property with these proceeds, move in, and repeat the process.*

Whether you take the "safe and easy" plan or the "bootstrap" plan, you'll get there. Both ways work. Just be diligent in continuing to upgrade your units. Keep an eye on market rents. Follow the guidelines I've laid out in this book. Talk to other investors. Get a good mortgage broker. You can do this, I promise you. Stick to your strategy and you will meet, and likely exceed, your financial goals. Best of luck to you.

15

WHERE DO YOU GO
FROM HERE?

Whether you think you can or think you can't, you're right.

—Henry Ford

ADDITIONAL RESOURCES

Hopefully, after reading this book you feel you have enough information to get started. But you may need help on understanding financial aspects of investing, dealing with mortgage brokers, estimating the cost of rehabbing, getting contacts to contractors, or just finding a good broker. The following is a list of places to turn for more resources.

OTHER GOOD BOOKS

I'm a firm believer in learning from the wisdom and experience of others. Books are an inexpensive and easy way to glean new techniques, perspectives, and approaches. All books are not created equal, however. Some may be great books but are published by small publishing companies and may be harder to find (if so, search at *http://www.bn.com* or *http://www.amazon.com*). Other books may be published by recognized publishers but are written by authors with little or no actual experience. While I may not agree with everything authors say, these are the best books in each area that I have read.

General Real Estate
- Milt Tanzer, *Real Estate Investments and How to Make Them,* 3d ed. (Prentice Hall, 1996).
- Martin Stone and Spencer Strauss, *The Unofficial Guide to Real Estate Investing* (IDG Books Worldwide, 1999).

Single-Family, Rehab and Flip
- Kevin Myers, *Buy It, Fix It, Sell It, Profit!* 2d ed. (Dearborn Trade Publishing, 2003).

Single-Family, Low-End ("Ugly Houses"), Rehab and Hold
- Jay Decima, *Start Small, Profit Big in Real Estate* (McGraw-Hill, 2005).

Buy-and-Hold Strategy
- David Schumacher, *Buy and Hold* (Schumacher Enterprises, 2004).

Tax-Deed Acquisitions (or Tax-Lien Purchases)
- Larry Loftis, *Profit by Investing in Real Estate Tax Liens* (Dearborn Trade Publishing, 2005).

Tenant Management
- Leigh Robinson, *Landlording,* 9th ed. (Express, 2001).

Commercial Multifamily (Apartments, Five Units and Up)
- Steve Berges, *Buying and Selling Apartment Buildings* (Wiley, 2005).

- Steve Berges, *The Complete Guide to Investing in Rental Properties* (McGraw-Hill, 2004).

Real Estate Finance
- Steve Berges, *The Complete Guide to Real Estate Finance for Investment Properties* (Wiley, 2004).

General Wealth Building
- Robert Kiyosaki, *Rich Dad, Poor Dad* (Tech Press, 1998).
- Robert Kiyosaki, *Cash Flow Quadrant* (Warner Business Books, 1999).
- Robert Kiyosaki, *Rich Dad's Prophecy* (Warner Business Books, 2002).
- Robert Kiyosaki, *Who Took My Money?* (Warner Business Books, 2004).
- Donald Trump, *The Art of the Deal* (Random House, 1987).
- Donald Trump, *How to Get Rich* (Random House, 2004).

WEB SITES

- *http://www.realtor.com.* Use its search engine (go to "more options") to find multifamily properties listed through MLS.
- *http://www.realestatejournal.com.* This is the online real estate section of the *Wall Street Journal.* Use the "Tool Kit" to find comparable sales for your prospective properties.
- *http://www.loopnet.com.* Loopnet is *the* place to look online for commercial properties. Sometimes you will find a quad or two listed here as well.
- *http://www.johntreed.com.* John Reed provides valuable and reliable information on most real estate subjects, and produces his own newsletter and publications on topics such as "Aggressive Tax Avoidance." I tend to agree with John 95

percent of the time, and the other 5 percent I respect his opinion as well considered.

REAL ESTATE CLUBS

The best place I've seen for getting practical help is at real estate clubs. Often their meetings are free (or they may have a minimal charge to cover the room rental) and their seminars are often well priced. You can go to *http://www.nationalreia.com* or *http://www.creonline.com* to find a club near you. Some clubs, like the one led by Robert Clark in Jacksonville, will provide substantial free training for new investors. If you are a new investor, go to as many of these meetings as you can. Eventually, you'll meet people who are experienced real estate investors. You'll also meet people who can provide services you need, such as contractors, mortgage bankers, and brokers.

That's the good news. The bad news is that most clubs will not perform any due diligence on their speakers. As such, the "expert" teacher could be someone who has a product to sell, but has never closed any deals personally (or very few). Check out the speakers carefully before paying to attend any seminar.

REAL ESTATE SEMINARS

A handful of companies produce seminars around the country. You will recognize them by their late-night infomercials or full-page newspaper ads. Having lectured for some of these companies, I know how they operate and cannot recommend them. Here's how it works. The ad will tell you to come to a "workshop" to learn how to become rich. Typically, something of perceived value (like CDs or a digital camera) will be given away free as an additional draw to get more people into the seats. It's not a workshop; it's a sales pitch. The axiom "You don't get something for nothing" is certainly true.

Why would a company spend $60,000 to $100,000 in advertising (a full-page ad in a city newspaper is $20,000 or more, and generally runs three to six times), rent a hotel room, and fly in a staff of six people if there weren't a payoff? The payoff is that the company will get 10 to 20 percent of the attendees to an initial training. And at $995 to $1,500 for a two-day training or a $3,000 to $5,000 for a "boot camp" (a three-day training), this can be quite lucrative. Attendees receive training but are also strongly pitched on more products (often on more boot camps).

Don't get me wrong. I've attended many seminars, and I've taught many around the country. You can always learn something new from other investors. However, from what I've seen, virtually none of the "front-end" speakers with these big seminar companies is a real estate investor (they are on the road 4 to 15 days at a time), and *maybe* 5 percent of the people who teach at the camps are real estate investors.

Second, the boot camps produced by the seminar companies are notoriously overpriced and oversold. Typically, these training sessions cost $3,000 to $5,000 for a three-day event. At the event, the sponsors try to sell you on "mentoring," products, or more camps. Many of them have no problem selling an elderly widow on $15,000 to $20,000 worth of training and products. Everyone working the event gets a commission on all sales.

Seminars are great if:

1. They are reasonably priced.
2. You know who your instructor will be *before* you pay.
3. Your instructor has substantial, proven real estate experience (you will probably never see an attorney or CCIM as an instructor, or even a full-time investor).

4. You can *verify* your instructor's experience or past deals before you pay for the seminar. At the very least, ask for addresses of properties that he or she has bought or sold. With an address, you can search your county appraiser's Web site to verify the owner.

So, when you see those infomercials or those full-page ads, remember, *caveat emptor*—"buyer beware." If you answer an initial pitch, you should ask, "Who is behind this seminar?" When you are told "XYZ Corporation," ask, "And who is behind XYZ? Who is the main shareholder?" If they don't tell you, that's a red flag. Many of the promoters hide behind layers of companies because they have questionable reputations. If you want to see who those people are, a great Web site to check is *http://www.johntreed.com.* John Reed is an experienced real estate investor and a West Point grad, and has an MBA from Harvard. Go to the real estate section and click on "Guru Ratings." You'll be amazed at what you find.

REAL ESTATE APPRECIATION BY METROPOLITAN AREA

FIGURE A.I *Appreciation by MSA and Divisions*

Rankings by
*Metropolitan Statistical Areas and Divisions Percent
Change in House Prices with MSA Rankings**
Period Ended June 30, 2005

MSA	National Ranking**	1-Yr.	Qtr.	5-Yr.
Akron, OH	238	4.37	1.51	21.72
Albany-Schenectady-Troy, NY	60	18.24	6.05	65.20
Albuquerque, NM	99	11.83	4.92	32.46
Allentown-Bethlehem-Easton, PA-NJ	70	16.93	5.64	58.23
Amarillo, TX	203	5.28	1.88	21.93
Anchorage, AK	85	14.51	3.47	46.37
Anderson, IN	206	5.13	0.43	18.21
Anderson, SC	256	2.69	-0.82	20.44
Ann Arbor, MI	172	6.29	2.68	31.13
Appleton, WI	191	5.60	0.48	25.35
Asheville, NC	113	10.22	1.57	39.92
Athens-Clarke County, GA	201	5.31	0.76	32.17
Atlanta-Sandy Springs-Marietta, GA	200	5.32	0.80	28.12
Atlantic City, NJ	38	23.51	8.07	95.77
Augusta-Richmond County, GA-SC	163	6.71	2.78	29.38
Austin-Round Rock, TX	207	5.07	3.02	20.84
Bakersfield, CA	2	33.88	5.79	114.63
Baltimore-Towson, MD	43	22.32	5.24	83.45
Barnstable Town, MA	98	12.04	1.43	95.25
Baton Rouge, LA	219	4.78	1.71	21.58
Battle Creek, MI	259	2.53	-1.71	24.46
Bay City, MI	241	4.13	0.56	26.06
Beaumont-Port Arthur, TX	211	4.97	3.04	22.82
Bellingham, WA	42	22.67	6.84	69.30
Bend, OR	72	16.61	6.05	56.54
Bethesda-Frederick-Gaithersburg, MD (MSAD)	40	23.21	6.10	96.96
Billings, MT	101	11.67	4.71	40.98

*For composition of metropolitan statistical areas and divisions see
http://www.census.gov/population/estimates/metro-city/0312msa.txt
or see OFHEO HPI FAQ #8 for more information.

**Note: Rankings based on annual percentage change, for all MSAs containing at least 15,000
transactions over the last 10 years.

FIGURE A.I   *Appreciation by MSA and Divisions (Continued)*

Rankings by
*Metropolitan Statistical Areas and Divisions Percent
Change in House Prices with MSA Rankings**
Period Ended June 30, 2005

MSA	National Ranking**	1-Yr.	Qtr.	5-Yr.
Birmingham-Hoover, AL	137	8.11	2.27	29.79
Blacksburg-Christiansburg-Radford, VA	106	11.42	3.61	39.44
Bloomington, IN	194	5.55	0.24	27.04
Bloomington-Normal, IL	234	4.46	2.29	18.95
Boise City-Nampa, ID	117	10.05	4.01	32.99
Boston-Quincy, MA (MSAD)	102	11.62	2.09	74.67
Boulder, CO	220	4.77	0.96	27.55
Bowling Green, KY	176	6.13	2.43	20.39
Bremerton-Silverdale, WA	57	19.39	5.55	59.03
Bridgeport-Stamford-Norwalk, CT	83	15.07	3.60	67.03
Buffalo-Niagara Falls, NY	210	4.97	0.65	27.75
Burlington, NC	252	3.28	0.06	16.48
Burlington-South Burlington, VT	80	15.62	3.55	58.50
Cambridge-Newton-Framingham, MA (MSAD)	110	11.14	2.67	59.53
Camden, NJ (MSAD)	69	17.09	3.83	74.73
Canton-Massillon, OH	254	2.83	0.60	20.52
Cape Coral-Fort Myers, FL	9	29.84	9.82	106.99
Cedar Rapids, IA	237	4.37	0.47	21.09
Champaign-Urbana, IL	160	6.85	2.04	30.42
Charleston, WV	227	4.60	1.86	19.58
Charleston-North Charleston, SC	71	16.87	4.16	49.21
Charlotte-Gastonia-Concord, NC-SC	246	3.75	0.35	18.22
Charlottesville, VA	52	19.86	5.89	68.89
Chattanooga, TN-GA	149	7.65	2.47	30.71
Cheyenne, WY	130	8.83	1.42	40.28
Chicago-Naperville-Joliet, IL (MSAD)	107	11.31	2.83	47.20
Chico, CA	36	23.97	6.06	114.17

*For composition of metropolitan statistical areas and divisions see
http://www.census.gov/population/estimates/metro-city/0312msa.txt
or see OFHEO HPI FAQ #8 for more information.

**Note: Rankings based on annual percentage change, for all MSAs containing at least 15,000
transactions over the last 10 years.

FIGURE A.1   *Appreciation by MSA and Divisions (Continued)*

Rankings by
*Metropolitan Statistical Areas and Divisions Percent
Change in House Prices with MSA Rankings**
Period Ended June 30, 2005

MSA	National Ranking**	1-Yr.	Qtr.	5-Yr.
Cincinnati-Middletown, OH-KY-IN	198	5.50	1.20	23.73
Cleveland-Elyria-Mentor, OH	228	4.56	1.01	22.77
Coeur d'Alene, ID	14	28.98	8.12	59.90
Colorado Springs, CO	146	7.75	2.48	32.89
Columbia, MO	134	8.35	2.46	25.59
Columbia, SC	157	7.08	2.12	26.90
Columbus, GA-AL	135	8.33	1.94	29.80
Columbus, IN	232	4.50	0.90	16.81
Columbus, OH	193	5.56	1.23	24.54
Dallas-Plano-Irving, TX (MSAD)	250	3.40	1.24	21.36
Davenport-Moline-Rock Island, IA-IL	216	4.85	0.65	24.73
Dayton, OH	224	4.67	0.80	19.50
Deltona-Daytona Beach-Ormond Beach, FL	31	24.94	7.20	90.99
Denver-Aurora, CO	239	4.35	0.84	29.01
Des Moines, IA	173	6.28	1.85	27.64
Detroit-Livonia-Dearborn, MI (MSAD)	249	3.41	0.48	24.43
Dubuque, IA	218	4.78	0.58	24.97
Duluth, MN-WI	111	10.56	2.88	57.62
Durham, NC	183	5.91	1.76	23.84
Eau Claire, WI	156	7.15	2.34	30.56
Edison, NJ (MSAD)	62	17.72	4.31	88.46
Elkhart-Goshen, IN	213	4.92	0.25	18.20
El Paso, TX	136	8.29	2.42	26.56
Essex County, MA (MSAD)	112	10.55	1.61	66.16
Eugene-Springfield, OR	67	17.43	5.26	40.51
Evansville, IN-KY	217	4.81	0.71	20.61
Fargo, ND-MN	122	9.72	2.38	39.63

*For composition of metropolitan statistical areas and divisions see
http://www.census.gov/population/estimates/metro-city/0312msa.txt
or see OFHEO HPI FAQ #8 for more information.

**Note: Rankings based on annual percentage change, for all MSAs containing at least 15,000
transactions over the last 10 years.

FIGURE A.I   *Appreciation by MSA and Divisions (Continued)*

Rankings by
*Metropolitan Statistical Areas and Divisions Percent
Change in House Prices with MSA Rankings**
Period Ended June 30, 2005

MSA	National Ranking**	1-Yr.	Qtr.	5-Yr.
Fayetteville-Springdale-Rogers, AR-MO	100	11.74	2.72	40.27
Flagstaff, AZ-UT	48	21.44	6.15	65.22
Flint, MI	221	4.72	0.03	23.53
Florence, SC	229	4.56	0.08	23.93
Fond du Lac, WI	225	4.63	1.12	25.97
Fort Collins-Loveland, CO	236	4.42	1.18	30.51
Fort Lauderdale-Pompano Beach-Deerfield Beach, FL (MSAD)	20	26.93	6.87	115.85
Fort Wayne, IN	245	3.87	1.05	16.34
Fort Worth-Arlington, TX (MSAD)	247	3.61	1.29	21.31
Fresno, CA	19	27.01	5.94	123.6
Gainesville, GA	178	6.07	0.37	28.37
Gary, IN (MSAD)	168	6.50	1.54	24.23
Grand Junction, CO	121	9.75	3.15	42.38
Grand Rapids-Wyoming, MI	209	5.05	1.39	25.06
Greeley, CO	262	1.88	-0.01	28.75
Green Bay, WI	161	6.76	1.58	28.50
Greensboro-High Point, NC	253	3.17	-0.52	17.23
Greenville, SC	187	5.74	2.92	21.56
Gulfport-Biloxi, MS	141	7.91	2.76	26.10
Hagerstown-Martinsburg, MD-WV	33	24.54	6.76	75.08
Harrisburg-Carlisle, PA	129	8.85	2.87	32.19
Hartford-West Hartford-East Hartford, CT	104	11.53	2.25	53.80
Hickory-Lenoir-Morganton, NC	261	2.21	0.32	18.96
Holland-Grand Haven, MI	196	5.53	0.16	23.35
Honolulu, HI	29	25.22	6.39	83.71
Houston-Baytown-Sugar Land, TX	244	3.90	-0.14	24.66
Huntsville, AL	199	5.33	0.12	20.70

*For composition of metropolitan statistical areas and divisions see
http://www.census.gov/population/estimates/metro-city/0312msa.txt
or see OFHEO HPI FAQ #8 for more information.

**Note: Rankings based on annual percentage change, for all MSAs containing at least 15,000
transactions over the last 10 years.

FIGURE A.1   *Appreciation by MSA and Divisions (Continued)*

Rankings by
*Metropolitan Statistical Areas and Divisions Percent Change in House Prices with MSA Rankings**
Period Ended June 30, 2005

MSA	National Ranking**	1-Yr.	Qtr.	5-Yr.
Indianapolis, IN	235	4.42	1.32	19.95
Iowa City, IA	171	6.30	0.84	25.79
Jackson, MI	164	6.58	3.01	29.90
Jackson, MS	177	6.08	1.33	24.30
Jacksonville, FL	61	18.15	5.59	66.88
Janesville, WI	147	7.72	2.60	26.63
Jefferson City, MO	197	5.51	1.02	21.86
Joplin, MO	214	4.86	-0.34	25.66
Kalamazoo-Portage, MI	215	4.86	-0.62	25.58
Kankakee-Bradley, IL	153	7.30	3.14	25.33
Kansas City, MO-KS	180	5.98	1.18	29.62
Kennewick-Richland-Pasco, WA	184	5.80	2.71	31.31
Kingsport-Bristol-Bristol, TN-VA	119	9.87	3.71	30.49
Knoxville, TN	138	8.08	2.08	30.19
Kokomo, IN	263	1.08	0.29	14.65
La Crosse, WI-MN	148	7.68	1.42	32.66
Lafayette, IN	264	0.91	-1.10	10.88
Lafayette, LA	158	7.00	1.95	29.11
Lake County-Kenosha County, IL-WI (MSAD)	125	9.19	2.45	39.93
Lakeland, FL	58	19.36	6.03	56.71
Lancaster, PA	94	12.50	3.85	39.19
Lansing-East Lansing, MI	169	6.50	0.79	30.00
Las Vegas-Paradise, NV	21	26.91	4.38	96.09
Lawrence, KS	142	7.88	2.30	34.42
Lexington-Fayette, KY	181	5.97	1.68	26.40
Lima, OH	208	5.05	-0.15	25.93
Lincoln, NE	152	7.44	2.71	22.76

*For composition of metropolitan statistical areas and divisions see
http://www.census.gov/population/estimates/metro-city/0312msa.txt
or see OFHEO HPI FAQ #8 for more information.

**Note: Rankings based on annual percentage change, for all MSAs containing at least 15,000 transactions over the last 10 years.

FIGURE A.1 *Appreciation by MSA and Divisions (Continued)*

Rankings by
*Metropolitan Statistical Areas and Divisions Percent
Change in House Prices with MSA Rankings**
Period Ended June 30, 2005

MSA	National Ranking**	1-Yr.	Qtr.	5-Yr.
Little Rock-North Little Rock, AR	166	6.53	2.16	26.50
Logan, UT-ID	174	6.25	1.24	20.02
Longview, WA	115	10.16	4.20	26.51
Los Angeles-Long Beach-Glendale, CA (MSAD)	30	25.12	5.08	115.09
Louisville, KY-IN	195	5.55	1.15	25.04
Lynchburg, VA	128	9.08	3.02	32.71
Macon, GA	251	3.29	0.55	21.71
Madison, WI	114	10.17	2.17	39.32
Manchester-Nashua, NH	103	11.53	1.12	72.26
Mansfield, OH	265	0.44	-2.73	21.01
Medford, OR	24	26.23	6.44	86.89
Memphis, TN-MS-AR	242	4.11	1.24	18.13
Merced, CA	3	32.67	8.63	131.37
Miami-Miami Beach-Kendall, FL (MSAD)	34	24.39	6.51	107.94
Michigan City-La Porte, IN	257	2.67	-0.84	24.53
Milwaukee-Waukesha-West Allis, WI	109	11.18	2.53	41.82
Minneapolis-St. Paul-Bloomington, MN-WI	123	9.43	2.02	56.35
Missoula, MT	116	10.13	3.02	55.97
Mobile, AL	202	5.29	3.77	21.90
Modesto, CA	10	29.56	8.09	132.29
Monroe, MI	223	4.69	-0.53	24.49
Montgomery, AL	143	7.86	3.73	21.67
Muskegon-North Shores, MI	165	6.53	3.35	25.40
Myrtle Beach-Conway-North Myrtle Beach, SC	93	12.62	3.49	35.98
Napa, CA	53	19.70	3.40	102.38
Naples-Marco Island, FL	1	35.60	13.50	114.69
Nashville-Davidson-Murfreesboro, TN	144	7.85	2.54	25.24

*For composition of metropolitan statistical areas and divisions see
http://www.census.gov/population/estimates/metro-city/0312msa.txt
or see OFHEO HPI FAQ #8 for more information.

**Note: Rankings based on annual percentage change, for all MSAs containing at least 15,000
transactions over the last 10 years.

FIGURE A.I *Appreciation by MSA and Divisions (Continued)*

Rankings by
*Metropolitan Statistical Areas and Divisions Percent Change in House Prices with MSA Rankings**
Period Ended June 30, 2005

MSA	National Ranking**	1-Yr.	Qtr.	5-Yr.
Nassau-Suffolk, NY (MSAD)	68	17.14	3.59	92.35
Newark-Union, NJ-PA (MSAD)	64	17.48	3.52	74.38
New Haven-Milford, CT	89	14.12	2.94	68.04
New Orleans-Metairie-Kenner, LA	145	7.76	1.97	36.54
New York-Wayne-White Plains, NY-NJ (MSAD)	65	17.47	4.39	80.46
Niles-Benton Harbor, MI	179	6.01	1.21	32.86
Norwich-New London, CT	73	16.50	3.21	70.24
Oakland-Fremont-Hayward, CA (MSAD)	37	23.65	6.38	88.2
Ogden-Clearfield, UT	185	5.77	1.64	15.34
Oklahoma City, OK	167	6.52	2.32	29.66
Olympia, WA	59	18.72	7.53	49.72
Omaha-Council Bluffs, NE-IA	205	5.13	0.92	22.76
Orlando, FL	35	24.09	7.68	72.30
Oshkosh-Neenah, WI	222	4.71	0.02	25.87
Oxnard-Thousand Oaks-Ventura, CA	47	21.53	3.40	109.09
Palm Bay-Melbourne-Titusville, FL	5	31.45	6.60	110.25
Pensacola-Ferry Pass-Brent, FL	27	25.83	7.08	61.99
Peoria, IL	186	5.75	1.95	23.54
Philadelphia, PA (MSAD)	74	16.44	4.12	68.10
Phoenix-Mesa-Scottdale, AZ	7	30.48	10.90	67.31
Pittsburgh, PA	189	5.72	1.14	30.58
Portland-South Portland-Biddeford, ME	91	13.22	2.48	70.35
Portland-Vancouver-Beaverton, OR-WA	81	15.34	5.35	41.99
Port St. Lucie-Fort Pierce, FL	18	27.20	7.12	120.98
Poughkeepsie-Newburgh-Middletown, NY	78	15.71	1.96	87.05
Prescott, AZ	16	28.63	10.14	70.57
Providence-New Bedford-Fall River, RI-MA	79	15.67	3.65	96.14

*For composition of metropolitan statistical areas and divisions see
http://www.census.gov/population/estimates/metro-city/0312msa.txt
or see OFHEO HPI FAQ #8 for more information.

**Note: Rankings based on annual percentage change, for all MSAs containing at least 15,000 transactions over the last 10 years.

FIGURE A.I   *Appreciation by MSA and Divisions (Continued)*

Rankings by
*Metropolitan Statistical Areas and Divisions Percent
Change in House Prices with MSA Rankings**
Period Ended June 30, 2005

MSA	National Ranking**	1-Yr.	Qtr.	5-Yr.
Provo-Orem, UT	204	5.16	1.20	16.75
Pueblo, CO	182	5.96	3.45	28.64
Punta Gorda, FL	12	29.39	7.80	109.63
Racine, WI	97	12.20	1.54	40.38
Raleigh-Cary, NC	231	4.53	0.72	18.01
Reading, PA	86	14.45	3.19	45.12
Redding, CA	39	23.35	5.58	111.48
Reno-Sparks, NV	4	32.27	7.29	98.45
Richmond, VA	77	15.90	4.31	50.19
Riverside-San Bernardino-Ontario, CA	25	26.13	4.49	124.3
Roanoke, VA	131	8.81	1.38	34.95
Rochester, MN	175	6.21	0.60	30.86
Rochester, NY	243	4.08	1.63	21.79
Rockford, IL	140	8.00	1.43	25.80
Rockingham County-Strafford County, NH (MSAD)	96	12.32	2.69	68.78
Sacramento-Arden-Arcade-Roseville, CA	28	25.50	5.44	120.91
Saginaw-Saginaw Township North, MI	255	2.82	-1.47	21.73
St. Cloud, MN	120	9.77	2.51	50.45
St. George, UT	17	28.34	10.17	47.66
St. Louis, MO-IL	126	9.15	2.33	39.25
Salem, OR	124	9.38	2.63	28.44
Salinas, CA	23	26.36	3.09	112.23
Salt Lake City, UT	127	9.13	3.74	22.92
San Antonio, TX	139	8.07	3.08	28.37
San Diego-Carlsbad-San Marcos, CA	49	21.27	2.63	118.27
San Francisco-San Mateo-Redwood City, CA (MSAD)	55	19.65	5.32	62.08
San Jose-Sunnyvale-Santa Clara, CA	46	21.54	6.66	52.81

*For composition of metropolitan statistical areas and divisions see
http://www.census.gov/population/estimates/metro-city/0312msa.txt
or see OFHEO HPI FAQ #8 for more information.

**Note: Rankings based on annual percentage change, for all MSAs containing at least 15,000
transactions over the last 10 years.

FIGURE A.I *Appreciation by MSA and Divisions (Continued)*

Rankings by
*Metropolitan Statistical Areas and Divisions Percent Change in House Prices with MSA Rankings**
Period Ended June 30, 2005

MSA	National Ranking**	1-Yr.	Qtr.	5-Yr.
San Luis Obispo-Paso Robles, CA	54	19.68	3.13	108.5
Santa Ana-Anaheim-Irvine, CA (MSAD)	45	22.09	4.32	112.48
Santa Barbara-Santa Maria-Goleta, CA	22	26.66	4.81	127.98
Santa Cruz-Watsonville, CA	56	19.46	4.28	68.05
Santa Fe, NM	95	12.47	1.22	48.15
Santa Rosa-Petaluma, CA	50	21.26	4.35	85.99
Sarasota-Bradenton-Venice, FL	11	29.50	6.96	100.77
Savannah, GA	105	11.48	0.85	45.79
Scranton-Wilkes-Barre, PA	133	8.57	3.04	32.54
Seattle-Bellevue-Everett, WA (MSAD)	84	14.93	4.97	44.11
Sheboygan, WI	118	10.00	2.19	28.31
Shreveport-Bossier City, LA	132	8.59	2.54	31.12
Sioux Falls, SD	188	5.72	1.32	25.55
South Bend-Mishawaka, IN-MI	170	6.33	1.36	22.53
Spartanburg, SC	258	2.67	-1.08	16.35
Spokane, WA	76	15.91	5.66	39.26
Springfield, IL	226	4.61	0.81	17.07
Springfield, MA	88	14.17	2.29	65.80
Springfield, MO	154	7.23	1.39	25.09
Springfield, OH	155	7.21	4.78	24.14
Stockton, CA	6	31.14	7.37	120.73
Syracuse, NY	162	6.72	3.19	36.37
Tacoma, WA (MSAD)	63	17.53	4.77	53.86
Tallahassee, FL	82	15.32	3.55	54.35
Tampa-St. Petersburg-Clearwater, FL	51	21.24	5.59	79.75
Toledo, OH	230	4.55	1.32	25.00
Topeka, KS	151	7.52	2.95	30.44

*For composition of metropolitan statistical areas and divisions see
http://www.census.gov/population/estimates/metro-city/0312msa.txt
or see OFHEO HPI FAQ #8 for more information.

**Note: Rankings based on annual percentage change, for all MSAs containing at least 15,000 transactions over the last 10 years.

FIGURE A.I   *Appreciation by MSA and Divisions (Continued)*

Rankings by
*Metropolitan Statistical Areas and Divisions Percent Change in House Prices with MSA Rankings**
Period Ended June 30, 2005

MSA	National Ranking**	1-Yr.	Qtr.	5-Yr.
Trenton-Ewing, NJ	66	17.45	3.82	77.54
Tucson, AZ	44	22.26	8.31	61.39
Tulsa, OK	248	3.44	1.46	22.04
Tuscaloosa, AL	150	7.54	-0.04	26.53
Vallejo-Fairfield, CA	41	23.00	5.09	111.81
Virginia Beach-Norfolk-Newport News, VA-NC	32	24.60	6.25	76.44
Visalia-Porterville, CA	8	30.42	5.49	90.93
Warren-Farmington Hills-Troy, MI (MSAD)	240	4.24	0.65	23.44
Washington-Arlington-Alexandria, DC-VA-MD-WV (MSAD)	26	26.00	6.63	101.22
Waterloo-Cedar Falls, IA	192	5.59	3.35	32.40
Wausau, WI	190	5.67	0.67	30.90
Wenatchee, WA	92	12.66	5.32	30.72
West Palm Beach-Boca Raton-Boynton Beach, FL (MSAD)	15	28.83	6.68	113.92
Wichita, KS	260	2.50	0.96	20.64
Wilmington, DE-MD-NJ (MSAD)	75	16.24	3.82	62.48
Wilmington, NC	87	14.44	3.83	38.62
Winston-Salem, NC	233	4.50	0.52	18.97
Worcester, MA	108	11.27	2.08	72.64
Yakima, WA	159	6.87	2.67	22.48
York-Hanover, PA	90	13.97	3.68	39.30
Youngstown-Warren-Boardman, OH-PA	212	4.97	2.68	22.91
Yuba City, CA	13	29.09	7.34	131.86

*For composition of metropolitan statistical areas and divisions see
http://www.census.gov/population/estimates/metro-city/0312msa.txt
or see OFHEO HPI FAQ #8 for more information.

**Note: Rankings based on annual percentage change, for all MSAs containing at least 15,000 transactions over the last 10 years.

FIGURE A.2 *Appreciation by Unranked MSAs and Divisions*

Unranked Metropolitan Statistical Areas and Divisions*
Percent Change in House Prices for MSAs and
Divisions Not Ranked in Previous Tables**

Period Ended June 30, 2005

MSA	1-Yr.	5-Yr.**
Abilene, TX	6.09	23.81
Albany, GA	6.57	23.74
Alexandria, LA	4.40	22.52
Altoona, PA	5.52	27.68
Ames, IA	3.56	21.47
Anniston-Oxford, AL	7.32	29.16
Auburn-Opelika, AL	10.14	33.22
Bangor, ME	13.29	54.81
Binghamton, NY	10.23	30.39
Bismarck, ND	7.83	33.34
Brownsville-Harlingen, TX	7.44	26.44
Brunswick, GA	11.71	44.00
Carson City, NV	28.73	98.76
Casper, WY	15.89	55.43
Clarksville, TN-KY	7.96	25.53
Cleveland, TN	5.54	25.66
College Station-Bryan, TX	4.68	21.92
Corpus Christi, TX	8.55	32.96
Corvallis, OR	11.54	30.72
Cumberland, MD-WV	8.64	39.28
Dalton, GA	5.87	30.94
Danville, IL	9.26	29.74
Danville, VA	6.84	24.30
Decatur, AL	4.39	17.33

*For composition of metropolitan statistical areas and divisions see
http://www.census.gov/population/estimates/metro-city/0312msa.txt
or see OFHEO HPI FAQ #8 for more information.

Note: While these MSAs meet our minimum criteria for publication, indices are subject to more variability based on smaller sample sizes. As this variability is most pronounced in the last quarter, it is advised that the reader track these numbers for stability over the release of the next few HPI reports.

**Note: Blanks are displayed where statistical criteria is not met early enough to display the five-year percentage change.

FIGURE A.2 *Appreciation by Unranked MSAs and Divisions (Continued)*

Unranked Metropolitan Statistical Areas and Divisions*
Percent Change in House Prices for MSAs and Divisions Not Ranked in Previous Tables**

Period Ended June 30, 2005

MSA	1-Yr.	5-Yr.**
Decatur, IL	6.80	22.22
Dothan, AL	8.20	28.26
Dover, DE	21.72	55.24
El Centro, CA	31.97	85.18
Elizabethtown, KY	4.47	25.71
Elmira, NY	3.24	19.83
Erie, PA	4.53	22.28
Fairbanks, AK	13.34	36.83
Farmington, NM	15.31	46.05
Fayetteville, NC	6.27	19.24
Florence-Muscle Shoals, AL	4.19	16.46
Fort Smith, AR-OK	5.24	22.57
Fort Walton Beach-Crestview-Destin, FL	32.93	90.44
Gadsden, AL	8.26	31.32
Gainesville, FL	17.00	63.64
Glens Falls, NY	15.39	61.02
Goldsboro, NC	0.66	14.29
Grand Forks, ND-MN	11.31	36.73
Great Falls, MT	11.00	32.32
Greenville, NC	5.17	20.75
Hanford-Corcoran, CA	28.30	94.80
Harrisonburg, VA	17.58	47.50
Hattiesburg, MS	4.75	20.98
Hinesville-Fort Stewart, GA	8.81	.
Hot Springs, AR	6.70	27.32

*For composition of metropolitan statistical areas and divisions see
http://www.census.gov/population/estimates/metro-city/0312msa.txt
or see OFHEO HPI FAQ #8 for more information.

Note: While these MSAs meet our minimum criteria for publication, indices are subject to more variability based on smaller sample sizes. As this variability is most pronounced in the last quarter, it is advised that the reader track these numbers for stability over the release of the next few HPI reports.

**Note: Blanks are displayed where statistical criteria is not met early enough to display the five-year percentage change.

FIGURE A.2 *Appreciation by Unranked MSAs and Divisions (Continued)*

Unranked Metropolitan Statistical Areas and Divisions*
Percent Change in House Prices for MSAs and
Divisions Not Ranked in Previous Tables**

Period Ended June 30, 2005

MSA	1-Yr.	5-Yr.**
Houma-Bayou Cane-Thibodaux, LA	8.37	32.28
Huntington-Ashland, WV-KY-OH	5.86	27.27
Idaho Falls, ID	10.00	30.56
Ithaca, NY	12.12	49.78
Jackson, TN	3.35	12.76
Jacksonville, NC	10.03	31.79
Johnson City, TN	5.55	25.67
Johnstown, PA	3.54	28.09
Jonesboro, AR	1.28	14.90
Killeen-Temple-Fort Hood, TX	4.26	23.88
Kingston, NY	16.87	83.78
Lake Charles, LA	2.75	23.24
Laredo, TX	1.89	21.56
Las Cruces, NM	14.84	41.14
Lawton, OK	10.32	26.05
Lebanon, PA	3.50	26.29
Lewiston, ID-WA	14.30	36.49
Lewiston-Auburn, ME	14.65	59.02
Longview, TX	5.30	23.52
Lubbock, TX	4.59	25.78
Madera, CA	24.01	117.42
McAllen-Edinburg-Phar, TX	3.55	21.88
Midland, TX	6.95	25.92
Monroe, LA	2.87	25.23
Morgantown, WV	15.08	43.28

*For composition of metropolitan statistical areas and divisions see
http://www.census.gov/population/estimates/metro-city/0312msa.txt
or see OFHEO HPI FAQ #8 for more information.

Note: While these MSAs meet our minimum criteria for publication, indices are subject to more variability based on smaller sample sizes. As this variability is most pronounced in the last quarter, it is advised that the reader track these numbers for stability over the release of the next few HPI reports.

**Note: Blanks are displayed where statistical criteria is not met early enough to display the five-year percentage change.

FIGURE A.2 *Appreciation by Unranked MSAs and Divisions (Continued)*

Unranked Metropolitan Statistical Areas and Divisions*
Percent Change in House Prices for MSAs and
Divisions Not Ranked in Previous Tables**

Period Ended June 30, 2005

MSA	1-Yr.	5-Yr.**
Morristown, TN	7.27	22.52
Mount Vernon-Anacortes, WA	19.43	50.27
Muncie, IN	3.13	19.67
Ocala, FL	22.99	67.59
Ocean City, NJ	23.01	110.51
Odessa, TX	8.32	24.21
Owensboro, KY	1.46	13.86
Panama City-Lynn Haven, FL	28.99	85.25
Parkersburg-Marietta, WV-OH	7.27	24.37
Pascagoula, MS	7.03	25.09
Pine Bluff, AR	5.90	25.42
Pittsfield, MA	14.52	62.13
Pocatello, ID	8.17	25.03
Rapid City, SD	7.65	40.65
Rocky Mount, NC	2.26	16.18
Rome, GA	0.69	26.26
Salisbury, MD	21.98	63.88
San Angelo, TX	9.04	24.45
Sandusky, OH	3.79	24.35
Sherman-Denison, TX	5.96	25.46
Sioux City, IA-NE-SD	3.09	14.50
St. Joseph, MO-KS	5.86	27.97
State College, PA	10.80	35.70
Sumter, SC	4.93	27.36
Terre Haute, IN	2.35	20.06

*For composition of metropolitan statistical areas and divisions see
http://www.census.gov/population/estimates/metro-city/0312msa.txt
or see OFHEO HPI FAQ #8 for more information.

Note: While these MSAs meet our minimum criteria for publication, indices are subject to more variability based on smaller sample sizes. As this variability is most pronounced in the last quarter, it is advised that the reader track these numbers for stability over the release of the next few HPI reports.

**Note: Blanks are displayed where statistical criteria is not met early enough to display the five-year percentage change.

FIGURE A.2 *Appreciation by Unranked MSAs and Divisions (Continued)*

Unranked Metropolitan Statistical Areas and Divisions*
Percent Change in House Prices for MSAs and
Divisions Not Ranked in Previous Tables**

Period Ended June 30, 2005

MSA	1-Yr.	5-Yr.**
Texarkana, TX-Texarkana, AR	6.18	27.33
Tyler, TX	4.67	27.21
Utica-Rome, NY	6.84	34.05
Valdosta, GA	7.40	28.61
Vero Beach, FL	27.39	99.19
Victoria, TX	5.17	17.78
Vineland-Millville-Bridgeton, NJ	19.43	61.10
Waco, TX	4.21	26.37
Warner Robins, GA	6.03	22.98
Weirton-Steubenville, WV-OH	4.93	27.65
Wheeling, WV-OH	3.77	29.05
Wichita Falls, TX	4.23	23.33
Williamsport, PA	9.74	30.16
Winchester, VA-WV	27.16	89.41
Yuma, AZ	35.98	67.28

*For composition of metropolitan statistical areas and divisions see
http://www.census.gov/population/estimates/metro-city/0312msa.txt
or see OFHEO HPI FAQ #8 for more information.

Note: While these MSAs meet our minimum criteria for publication, indices are subject to more variability based on smaller sample sizes. As this variability is most pronounced in the last quarter, it is advised that the reader track these numbers for stability over the release of the next few HPI reports.

**Note: Blanks are displayed where statistical criteria is not met early enough to display the five-year percentage change.